Dale Earnhardt Jr.

Inside the Rise of a NASCAR Superstar

RON LEMASTERS JR. AND AL PEARCE

PHOTOGRAPHY BY NIGEL KINRADE

AND HAROLD HINSON

MOTORBOOKS

First published in 2006 by Motorbooks, an imprint of MBI Publishing Company, Galtier Plaza, Suite 200, 380 Jackson Street, St. Paul, MN 55101-3885 USA

MBI Publishing Company titles are also available at discounts in bulk quantity for industrial or sales-promotional use. For details write to Special Sales Manager at MBI Publishing Company, Galtier Plaza, Suite 200, 380 Jackson Street, St. Paul, MN 55101-3885 USA

Editor: Lee Klancher
Designer: Mandy Iverson

Printed in China

Library of Congress Cataloging-in-Publication Data

Lemasters, Ron.
   Dale Earnhardt Jr. : making gold out of dirt / text by Ron Lemasters
Jr. and Al Pearce ; photography by Nigel Kinrade and Harold Hinson.
      p. cm.
      ISBN-13: 978-0-7603-2780-7 (hardbound w/ jacket)
      ISBN-10: 0-7603-2780-7 (hardbound w/ jacket)
   1. Earnhardt, Dale, Jr. 2. Stock car drivers--United
States--Biography. I. Pearce, Al, 1942- II. Kinrade, Nigel. III.
Hinson, Harold. IV. Title.
GV1032.E19L45 2006
796.72092--dc22
                              2006024580

On the endpapers: Dale Earnhardt Jr. rips past the logo at Atlanta Motor Speedway in 2004. *Nigel Kinrade*

On the frontispiece: Dale Jr. at Dover in 2004. *Nigel Kinrade*

On the title page: Dale Jr. is one of NASCAR's elite drivers, but his authenticity is what resonates with the fans. *Nigel Kinrade*

On the contents page: Dale celebrating at Richmond in 2004. *Nigel Kinrade*

On the back cover:
Top: Dale Earnhardt Jr. racing against veteran driver Dave Marcis. *Nigel Kinrade*

CONTENTS

Introduction

INSIDE THE ICON

E VERY YEAR, Harris Interactive releases its list of the nation's "Favorite Sports Stars."

Every year for the past three, Dale Earnhardt Jr. has been on it. This is significant to fans of NASCAR for two reasons: first, it's a national list, and the winner this year was Tiger Woods, the pro golfer who revolutionized the game as a young man.

Second, this recognition cements Earnhardt's position as the favorite NASCAR driver of a generation. The only athletes ahead of Junior on the list, according to the Harris Poll, were Woods, basketball's Michael Jordan, football's Brett Favre, and baseball's Derek Jeter.

That is stout, no matter where you're from.

What is it about Dale Earnhardt Jr. that captivates us? Is it his name? His rock-and-roll, good-ol'-boy persona? His story?

If you look at it objectively, you'll realize that it's all three in varying degrees to different people.

This book takes a look at the man inside the red Budweiser racing suit through the eyes of friends, acquaintances, and even his famous father. You'll read about how he got started in the sport with the help of a longtime family friend and short-track fixture; how he struggled in street stocks and late models; and, finally, how he made it to the big time with a gentle nudge from his dad and uncle.

There was a time, believe it or not, when Junior expected to work for his father for the rest of his life, changing oil at the Chevrolet dealership, and earning the princely sum of $16,000 a year.

You'll read about how, through the help and comfort of his sister Kelley, he survived military school and overcame a painful shyness as a child to cast a big shadow on the world, and how he returned the favor in a most poignant and solemn manner.

From his penchant to be "all about the party" in his younger years, Junior grew up to be a shrewd and discerning businessman in his late twenties, and as he progresses through his career, the lessons learned at the feet of his father are coming to the fore.

Everybody knows about Dale Earnhardt Sr.'s death in 2001 and its aftermath, but very few people know exactly how it affected his son. Sure, there was public grief, but for the most part, what feelings were exhibited came as the natural runoff from a watershed event in any person's life.

An intensely private person, he did his mourning out of the public's view and went out to face the music every long and tedious day of that terrible season.

The legions of fans that were left adrift when Earnhardt Sr. was killed for the most part transferred their allegiance to his son, and while that is a wonderful thing in and of itself, the massive weight of expectation nearly crushed him.

Following his father's death, Junior went through a period where he questioned everything and anything, stacking up what he felt against what he knew and discerning answers known only to him and the few close friends he keeps.

Since that time, he has come to grips with his loss, and with the loss felt by Earnhardt Nation. He was expected to pick up the flag, fallen with his father, and keep on marching. By and large, he's done just that, though to the beat of a slightly different drummer.

Dealing with expectations is a large part of Dale Earnhardt Jr.'s makeup as a man, as a racer, and as the potential heir to the kingdom his father built by sheer force of will.

Watching Earnhardt Jr. now, as a 31-year-old superstar, one cannot help but remember his father at that same age. There are similarities, to be sure, but there are differences, too, and that in part is what is so intriguing.

From his first foray into racing—selling a go kart built by his brother Kerry to buy a street stock to race at Concord Motorsports Park—to his years of barnstorming the late model scene in the Carolinas and Virginia, Earnhardt Jr. had to make it on his own before he got much in the way of help from his father.

That's the way Dale Sr. did it, and if it was good enough for him, then it would be good enough for Junior. Can't really argue with the results, can you?

With his brother, Kerry, and sister, Kelley, racing alongside him, he didn't exactly mow down the competition in late models, but he learned a great deal about how race cars work—and how hard it was to make them work right.

These lessons continue to serve him well on the track, but what about off the track?

Still shy and somewhat uncomfortable with all the hoopla that seems to surround him 24/7, Earnhardt Jr. is still an icon of his age. More than that, he's an icon with feet in both his own generation and that of his father.

This book, which examines not so much what Junior has done on the track (though there's a good bit of that) but what he does and has done off it, seeks to bring a better understanding of the man that is Dale Earnhardt Jr. through the eyes and voices of friends whose paths crossed his along the way and whose wisdom and teaching remain with him even now.

—*Ron Lemasters Jr.*
June 2006

LIFE IN MILITARY SCHOOL

Dale Jr.'s time at the Oak Ridge Military Academy played in role in forming the man who won the Winston in 2000. *Harold Hinson*

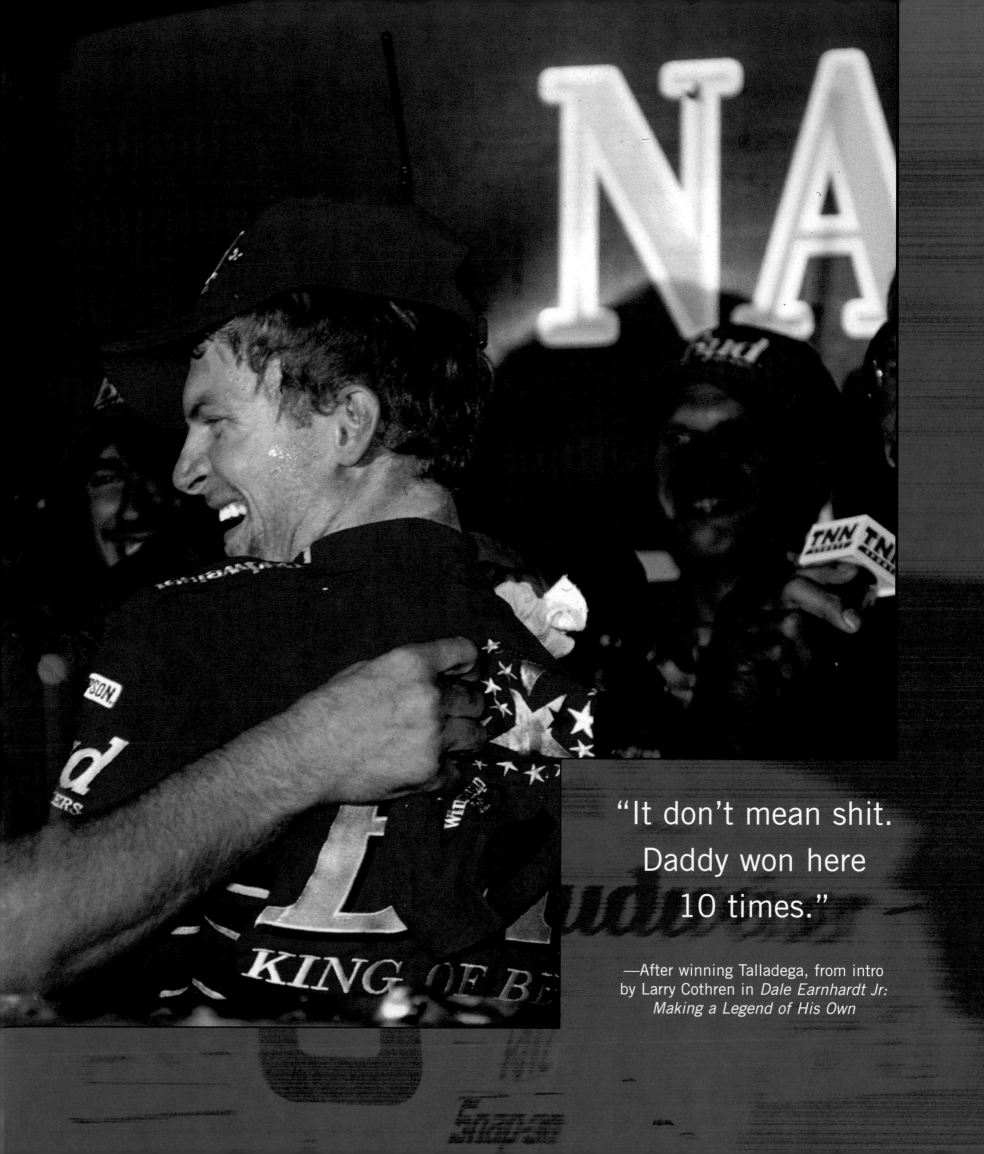

"It don't mean shit. Daddy won here 10 times."

—After winning Talladega, from intro by Larry Cothren in *Dale Earnhardt Jr: Making a Legend of His Own*

Nobody could ever accuse Dale Earnhardt Jr. of growing up a juvenile delinquent. High-spirited? Certainly. Fun loving? Absolutely. Well behaved? Most of the time. Academically motivated? Well, not always.

Clearly, there was something missing as Junior headed from grade school into his junior high school years in the early 1980s. His father was making the transition from a struggling driver to one of the biggest names in NASCAR, which meant his time was absorbed by the demands of being named the 1979 NASCAR Rookie of the Year and winning the 1980 series championship. Junior and his new stepmother, Teresa (she and Dale Earnhardt were married in 1982), weren't exactly the best of friends. After a series of minor incidents, he was asked to leave a private Christian grade school.

"But not for anything serious," Earnhardt Jr. said in an interview with NASCAR.com several years ago. "A couple of fights, talking in class, sleeping in class. That sort of thing got me dismissed. So [dad] and Teresa sent me to Oak Ridge Military Academy."

Opposite: The Earnhardts at the track in the late 1970s, a time when Dale Sr. was on the way to winning Rookie of the Year honors (1979) and his first Winston Cup title in 1980. *International Motorsports Hall of Fame*

Dale Jr. in March 2002, a time when his discipline and talent were paying off. That spring, he put together a string of top-five finishes at Atlanta, Darlington, and Martinsville. He capped that strong run with a win at Talladega on April 21, 2002. *Harold Hinson*

"Dad always said that before he met Teresa he owed the bank money," says Dale Earnhardt, Jr. in an interview with *MSNBC.com.* "And by the time they got married the bank owed him money."

The small private boarding school for boys and girls in grades 7–12 is in Oak Ridge, North Carolina, a crossroads community northwest of Greensboro in Guilford County. It's the country's third-oldest military high school and one of fewer than 100 such fully accredited, military-based high schools in the country. Perhaps jokingly—or perhaps not—Junior once said Oak Ridge Military Academy was home to "North Carolina's least likely to succeed."

(Jokingly or not, school officials take great exception to Junior's flippant comment. They point out with fervent enthusiasm that Oak Ridge is most definitely not a "reform school" or a training facility for undisciplined juvenile delinquents. They're proud of their long and admirable record of producing educated and productive young men and women).

Quakers founded Oak Ridge Male Academy as a "finishing school" in 1852. Two years later, it was renamed Oak Ridge Institute and began admitting girls. The school was closed during the Civil War and assumed its military structure in 1917. It reverted to its male-only posture and became Oak Ridge Military Institute in 1929. Girls were re-admitted and it was renamed yet again—this time to

Oak Ridge Academy—in 1971. Ten years later, the school assumed its current name of Oak Ridge Military Academy.

Its published goals are simple and no-nonsense: provide a disciplined environment; offer a safe, structured and caring environment for academic achievement and leadership training; teach students that choices carry consequences, and that individuals are responsible for those choices; espouse moral and ethical standards that are applied to daily life; and provide an environment where peer pressure works towards education and an atmosphere where academic achievement is valued.

By any measure, Earnhardt Jr. couldn't be considered an exceptional cadet or an outstanding student during his 18 months at Oak Ridge (parts of 1987 and 1988). On the other hand, he was never a serious problem, either. "I never made it past the rank of corporal, which wasn't much at all," he said in an interview several years ago. "They didn't necessarily hand out higher rank like Kleenex, but half of the population there was to be saluted or, guess what . . . 'Here, have a demerit, Junior.'"

But perhaps he's being too hard on himself. Coach/teacher Bobby Barbera is the only member of the current Oak Ridge faculty who was there during Earnhardt Jr.'s time. Barbera remembers him as "pretty much a normal seventh-grade cadet."

Junior in June 2003, a respectable month for Dale. He netted a solid 7th at Michigan, 4th at Pocono, and scored an 11th place on the road course at Sears Point. *Harold Hinson*

As Barbera explains, "I was the commandant of cadets, and Dale Jr. basically stayed out of trouble. In fact, he received the Commandant's Award for accumulating fewer than 10 demerits in a year. He played one year of junior high basketball and I named him to be the seventh-grade observer on the Honor Court, which handled all violations of the school's honor code."

The short period at Oak Ridge Military Academy might have been the only time Dale Earnhardt Jr. has ever been treated like everybody else. Barbera said the expectations for the Intimidator's son were the same as for everyone else at the school. "They got up at 6:30 a.m. and went to bed at 10 p.m., when 'Taps' was blown," he said. "He had to shine his shoes; polish his brass; send out and pick up his laundry; eat all his meals in the mess hall; and was required to study two hours at his desk each night from Sunday through Thursday. He did an adequate job as a student, maintaining about a C+ average.

"I remember Dale Sr. picking him up once (for weekend leave) and Teresa picking him up once. To the best of my memory, though, people from the (race) shop did most of the transporting. I think Dale Sr. attended one parade, but kept a very low profile."

Dale Jr. celebrates a win at Talladega in 2003. *Harold Hinson*

To many of NASCAR's younger fans, Earnhardt Jr.'s weekday routine sounds like a dreadful existence. There was the early wake-up call for morning formation and breakfast. There were the eight hours of

intense classroom work. There was "free time" from 3 p.m. to 6 p.m. (usually for study or taking care of personal issues), then dinner and a strictly enforced two-hour study period. There was another one-hour break before "lights out" at 10 p.m.

"Each day, your shoes had to be gleaming as brightly as your brass and any medals you may have received," Junior says in an interview about his days at Oak Ridge. "It was a simple routine, but if you failed at any of it or didn't follow exactly the rules the academy had laid out, you were handed a demerit. A demerit was something you had to work off. If you didn't, you weren't permitted to leave school for the weekend. In most cases, many kids didn't mind staying instead of spending the weekend at home. I found out quickly that if you did leave, it made it harder to come back.

"I spent one-and-a-half years at Oak Ridge, which was relatively short compared to most kids. But it was a crucial turning point in my life. The whole purpose of having some free time (and the military discipline) was to learn to take care of yourself. I'll always believe I was ten times the person after that experience. Good and bad, it made me smarter, stronger, and less likely to get my ass kicked. I knew more than the guy up the street who hadn't been to military school. I was more like an adult."

Which, according to Humpy Wheeler of Lowe's Motor Speedway, was exactly what Teresa and Dale Earnhardt had in mind when they sent him there. Wheeler, president and general manager of the track near Charlotte, knew the late Ralph Earnhardt, became very close to Dale Earnhardt Sr., and is a big fan of Dale Earnhardt Jr. In his mind, Junior's time at Oak Ridge exposed him to the discipline his father and step-mother couldn't provide at that time.

"Junior wasn't a bad kid growing up, not in any way at all," Wheeler says. "His father called me one day to talk about sending Junior away to military school. Because of the racing and everything that was going on right then, Dale and Teresa weren't home very much, not as much as they wanted to be. It worried Dale that he wasn't around for his children (Kerry, Dale Jr., and Kelley). He was big on discipline—everybody knows that—so he thought military school might help Junior.

"And I think it did. I've talked with Junior about it and I know he got a lot of good out of it. He joked to me one day about learning how to make a bed while he was there . . . But he's a really good guy, and I'm sure Oak Ridge helped him grow into the man he is."

From Oak Ridge, Junior began his freshman year at Mooresville High School (MHS) in 1988. Despite being the son of a multi-time NASCAR champion and the sport's most popular driver, Junior didn't feel the love at MHS. "For some reason, that worked against me," he said. "It wasn't cool to be Dale Earnhardt's son. I wasn't one of the preps or the jocks. I was too small for football, so I played soccer my freshman year. We went to the nationals every year, so the soccer guys were popular. But even when I was on the team, I wasn't one of them, couldn't be.

"Looking at them walking around in their polo shirts with their collars buttoned up—I thought they were a bunch of idiots." ●

"Junior wasn't a bad kid growing up,
not in any way at all.
His father called me one day to talk about
sending Junior away to military school.
Because of the racing and everything
that was going on right then,
Dale and Teresa weren't home very much,
not as much as they wanted to be.
It worried Dale that he wasn't around for his children
(Kerry, Dale Jr., and Kelley).
He was big on discipline—everybody knows that—
so he thought military school might help Junior."

—*Humpy Wheeler*

2

GOING SHORT-TRACK RACING AT MYRTLE BEACH

Dale's short track experience was anything but easy, with his Dad making sure he had mediocre equipment and very little help wrenching on his wrecks. Those formative years spent working on cars late into the night played a role in making Dale one of NASCAR's premier drivers. *Harold Hinson*

"Right from the get-go,
I saw that he was
in total control."

—Gary Hargett

MYRTLE BEACH SPEEDWAY (MBS) IS A HALF-MILE, moderately banked bullring near South Carolina's favorite resort city. Built and opened in 1958, it hosted nine dirt-track Grand National races (later called Winston Cup and currently Nextel Cup) over the next eight years. It was paved in 1971, but alternated between dirt and asphalt several times between then and 1987. Once it was repaved for good and upgraded, MBS became a Saturday night fixture for drivers working up the NASCAR ladder. Among them was a quiet, shy, red-headed teenager named Ralph Dale Earnhardt Jr.

After graduating from Mooresville High School in 1991, he'd spent two years getting an associate degree in automotive technology at the Kannapolis, North Carolina, campus of Mitchell Community College. (He jokingly called it MIT—Mitchell In Town). He also worked briefly in the service department of his father's Chevrolet dealership, changing oil. All the while, he and half-brother Kerry were scraping up enough money to convert a junked 1978 Chevrolet Monte Carlo into a race car.

In 1992, Junior reached the first major crossroad of his racing career. During a Friday night Street Stock race at Concord, North Carolina, he caught the eye of Gary Hargett, a longtime family friend and legendary car builder/crew chief. It didn't take Hargett long to realize that this third-generation racer might be as good as the other two Earnhardts he'd worked with through the years. To him, it seemed obvious he was the man to guide Junior's early steps toward the Nextel Cup.

After all, Hargett had raced against dirt-track legend Ralph Earnhardt (Junior's grandfather) in the 1950s and 1960s. He quit driving to concentrate on building and maintaining cars, and eventually became his old rival's crew chief. "I knew Ralph about my whole life and I knew Dale Earnhardt all his life," says Hargett, a short-track fixture for more than 50 years. "We raced in different classes, but I went wherever Ralph was so I could watch and learn from him. He built my first 'store-bought' car in the early '60s. Until then, I'd always turned junkyard cars into race cars. Ralph built me a car from the ground up. I was around him a lot, so I watched Big Dale grow up and become a racer."

At Concord that night, Hargett noticed 17-year-old Dale Earnhardt Jr. ran every lap wide open . . . but not recklessly so. "Right from the get-go, I saw that he was in total control," Hargett says. "He had a

Dale's short-track experience at Myrtle Beach taught him the value of working on your own car and how to drive a car under heavy pressure from unyielding competitors. *International Motorsports Hall of Fame*

big motor and was on street tires, so sometimes he got sideways. But he was always fast and never got in big trouble. I could see he had natural talent, something special inside him. To me, people with natural talent get out of messes without knowing how they did it. The rough talent was there all along; it just needed somebody to file it down."

Hargett told Dale Earnhardt that Junior was ready for the faster, tougher, more competitive late model stock car circuit. The father disagreed, saying he didn't think his son was good enough. Certainly, he argued, not old enough or experienced enough to move up. "We argued about it for a month or two," Hargett recalls. "Dale didn't think Junior was ready, but I did. We fought about it like cats and dogs. He was as hard-headed against as I was hard-headed for it. The first time we talked about it, Dale wondered if I knew which son was which. He thought I was talking about Kerry. I said, 'No, Dale, I know which one I'm talking about.' I thought Junior could be pretty good."

A few weeks later, Hargett was summoned to Earnhardt's small Busch Series shop in the original Dale Earnhardt Inc. complex in Mooresville. Junior was working there, learning the ins and outs of the racing business while running his Street Stock at Concord. According to Hargett, the conversation went something like this.

Earnhardt: Junior, this man wants you to drive his race car. Do you want to?

Junior (without looking up from what he was doing): Yes.

"That was it," Hargett says. "Junior didn't get excited or even look up. But it was different as soon as his father left. Junior got all excited as we talked about it. It's like he was so scared of his father that he didn't want to stop working or act excited. It was different when his father left. Junior was all excited and ready to go when it was just the two of us talking."

The future Nextel Cup star began his late model career at Myrtle Beach in the spring of 1993. He finished fifth in points behind Kevin Prince, Sean Graham, Edward Jordan, and Raymond Mason Jr. He had nine top-10s and was the division's Rookie of the Year. He was third in points in the next year, finishing behind veterans Charles Powell III and Graham. He got his first victory on August 20, 1994, and backed it with eight other top-10s. In 1995, he strung together nine top-fives en route to finishing fourth in points behind Powell III, Prince, and Graham. By then, the senior Dale Earnhardt was a seven-time NASCAR champion and the sport's most overwhelming force.

"And the thing is, Junior didn't have a really good car until his third season," Hargett says. "He raced older cars that I'd built the first two years, until his father decided he might be a racer after all. That's when he said to order a new late model from Rick Townsend up in Virginia. His father paid for tires and motors, but we had to win enough each weekend to take care of everything else. I used to borrow money from the bank on Fridays and hope to make enough to pay them back on Mondays. Really, we never had as much money as the late model teams we raced against. People might not believe it, but we did it the hard way."

Without question, Earnhardt Jr.'s best season was 1996. He finished second in Myrtle Beach Speedway points, 48 behind Powell III. Earnhardt Jr. had two

Young Dale at the track. Getting good backing was never a problem for Junior. *Harold Hinson*

Dale wore his Dad's number during his early years of racing. He'd have to earn the right to run his own number later in life.
Harold Hinson

victories and a phenomenal 23 other top-5s, a tribute to his consistency and uncanny ability to finish what he started. He also branched out that year, running a full late model stock car schedule on Friday nights at Florence Motor Speedway. There, he was fifth in points behind Jamey Lee, Ruby Branham, Robert Powell, and Glenn Smith.

But that season marked a bittersweet split with Hargett. Since their pairing in 1993, the legendary owner/coach and his young project had raced out of Hargett's shop in Marshville, North Carolina, a hamlet just off Route 74 between Monroe and Rockingham. Eventually, Dale Earnhardt wanted his son and Hargett to move everything to the new DEI headquarters in Mooresville. Hargett felt Junior was better served in Marshville, off the beaten path and isolated from the pressure of being the Intimidator's son.

"It was 72 miles from my shop to DEI and I wasn't going to make that trip every day," Hargett explains. "Besides, it wouldn't have worked as well at DEI. There were Cup and Busch cars there, and Kerry was there, and I didn't think it would work with those people telling Junior what to do and how to do it.

"I wanted to keep things under my roof, just the two of us, away from everything else. I thought things would be better at my shop. I didn't think he'd be able to develop at DEI. His father and I talked about it and he finally said, 'Do you need a job or not?' I said, 'Yeah, I need a job, but it doesn't have to be with you.' So they came and loaded everything and took it to Mooresville. That was the last time I had anything to do with Junior's career."

But those Friday and Saturday night bullring races gave Dale Earnhardt Jr. the elementary on-track education that still serves him well. He once described late model racing like building a remote-control car and taking it where everybody else was playing. He said racing at Myrtle Beach, Florence, and Nashville taught him to conserve his equipment, keep some hot laps in his tires, pace himself, and avoid the inevitable wrecks. He honed his communication and motivational skills, and learned how to get along with his rivals.

By all accounts, he was just one of the boys during those hot and muggy weekends. No camera crews. No agents or handlers. No inquiring (and annoying) members of the media dogging his every step. He was, instead, simply a young racer trying to make his own way in the increasingly long shadow cast by his famous father. Fellow late model racer Mike Dillon, now an executive at Richard Childress Racing, says Earnhardt Jr. was treated like everybody else. "The times I was there, the officials were pretty much sticklers for the rules," Dillon says. "They didn't give anybody any unfair breaks. Everybody had to follow the same rules, including him. I don't remember him ever getting any unfair advantage from the officials. Quite frankly, he wasn't always all that fast, so I don't see how they would have been giving him anything.

"If he had any advantage at all, it was that he had more sponsorship than the rest of us. All three of them, him, Kerry, and (sister) Kelley, had more backing at that level. They had Mom 'n Pop Stores and Chevrolet and SunDrop, really good deals like that. When you have that much sponsorship at that level, you can pretty much do anything."

Dillon remembers that Earnhardt Jr. didn't come rolling in with a big hauler filled with cars, parts, and pieces. He didn't have a large crew or engineers and specialists. His car was attractive and well maintained, but not obsessively so. "Dale didn't put him in the good equipment he could have," Dillon says. "My equipment was far superior to Junior's. I had three full-time people building and maintaining my stuff; his people were just weekend racers. I wondered why Dale did that, why he didn't let Junior have better stuff. He made Junior pull the frame and straighten the chassis when he wrecked. When I wrecked, I'd go get a new clip and put it on. I think Dale did that to make sure everybody knew Junior didn't have an unfair advantage. I think he would have had a lot more success if he'd had the equipment I did."

Former late model rival Ricky Dennis concurs. He's the son of Bill Dennis, winner of three consecutive Busch Series 300s in Daytona Beach and the 1970 Nextel Cup Rookie of the Year. Ricky's resume is

"Right from the get-go,
I saw that he was in total control.
He had a big motor and was on street tires,
so sometimes he got sideways.
But he was always fast and never got in big trouble.
I could see he had natural talent,
something special inside him.
To me, people with natural talent
get out of messes without knowing how they did it.
The rough talent was there all along;
it just needed somebody to file it down."

—*Gary Hargett*

impressive in its own right: late model driver, car builder at Townsend Race Cars in Virginia, former crew chief for several drivers, and promoter of the Arena Racing Series. He met Earnhardt Jr. for the first time in the early 1990s at a short track in North Carolina.

"I think Big Dale gave him lesser equipment so Junior would have to work on it to make it better," Dennis says. "Oh, sure, there were people jealous of him, saying he'd gotten this break or that. But I never saw it when I was around. I think the first really good late model he had was a Townsend car. Before that, he had to make do with stuff that wasn't all that great."

Dennis remembers one more thing about Earnhardt Jr. "He was serious and absolutely dedicated to racing," he says. "He worked on race cars day and night. Not only his cars, but on Kerry's and Kelley's, too. He had the desire and the determination to work his way up. It was almost like he had a vision for the future, that he could see where everything was going. I never saw him trying to use his name to get anything. If anything, it seemed like he wanted to make it on his own. That's how serious he was." ●

Dale Junior, Dale Senior, and Kerry Earnhardt. *Harold Hinson*

Opposite: Dale Junior at Texas Motor Speedway. *Harold Hinson*

3

THE DALE JR. MARKETING MACHINE

When it comes to representing a brand, Dale Jr. is one of the pack leaders. Here at Martinsville in 2004, he's on his way to a third-place finish. Race winner Rusty Wallace is lurking a few cars back, while Jimmie Johnson stayed on Earnhardt's and finished fourth. *Nigel Kinrade*

"He's genuine. . . .
He's NASCAR's
most popular driver
because he's real."

— Kathy Casso, Director, Budweiser's
domestic sport-related marketing

To some extent, Dale Earnhardt Jr. can thank Carl Kiekhaefer for helping make him an instantly recognizable and well-paid corporate spokesman. And while Junior's at it, he can also thank Donnie Allison, Cale Yarborough, and CBS-TV for helping pave the way for him to grow rich beyond any boyhood dream

Time was when motorsports sponsorship and marketing were primitive. To be sure, drivers have always needed OPM (other people's money) to go racing. They were delighted to take a few dollars to wear a hat or T-shirt promoting the corner grocer or neighborhood mechanic. But not until Kiekhaefer came along more than 50 years ago did anyone pay serious attention to racing marketing.

Kiekhaefer used stock car racing to market his line of Mercury outboard motors. He plastered "Mercury Outboards" on Dodges and Chryslers for many of NASCAR's best drivers, including Tim, Bob, and Fonty Flock; Buck Baker; Speedy Thompson; Jack Smith; Frank Mundy; Norm Nelson, and Herb Thomas. In 1955, the Kiekhaefer juggernaut won 22 races, and lead driver Tim Flock won the Grand National (later, Winston Cup and now Nextel Cup) title. In 1956, his drivers won 30 more races and Baker took the series championship. Then, stung by criticism that his teams were too good—and perhaps convinced that he'd made "Mercury Outboards" a household name—Kiekhaefer quit racing and went back to Wisconsin. For those 15 years, nobody came close to using racing as Kiekhaefer had.

Fast forward to the 1970s, when STP, Coca-Cola, Gatorade, and Purolator became sponsorship fixtures. Tuborg, Falstaff, Stroh's, and Carling became the sport's first beer sponsors. Some good teams had corporate backing—Petty, the Wood Brothers, Holman-Moody, and Junior Johnson—but only a handful of others had what could be considered major support.

The sponsorship and marketing landscape changed dramatically in February of 1979 when Allison and Yarborough repeatedly crashed each other on the last lap of the Daytona 500. In those 30 seconds or so, CBS telecast-delivered stock car racing squarely into America's consciousness. Almost overnight, Fortune 500 companies saw that millions of NASCAR fans would embrace any product associated with their favorite sport. It wasn't long before airlines, soft drinks, beers, clothing lines, tobacco products, fast-food chains, automotive products and household goods began appearing on cars. By the mid- to late-1980s, sponsorship and marketing had become integral parts of every team.

That was the atmosphere when Earnhardt Jr. moved from Late Models into the Busch Series for the 1998 and 1999 seasons. His Dale Earnhardt Inc.–owned No. 3 Chevrolets were backed by AC Delco, a cousin of his father's No. 3 GM Goodwrench Chevy in the Cup. After winning two Busch titles, Junior went Cup racing in 2000 with backing from Budweiser, one of NASCAR's longest-running and most visible "partners."

Kathy Casso is the director of Budweiser's domestic sport-related marketing. She recalls the company's all-out effort to convince Junior to drive for them as a rookie in 2000. While stopping short of saying Anheuser-Busch offered him the keys to the vault, she made it clear the company wanted him badly. And why not?

"He'd proven himself by winning two Busch championships, he had that great last name, and we felt he'd bring great credibility to our team," she said from her office in St. Louis. "We saw great potential for crossover appeal between racing and the 21- to 34-year-old beer drinkers. We felt he'd be the perfect representative for that group because he drinks beer, likes music, and he's really good in the race car."

But it's more than just that. After all, plenty of other 20- and 30-something drivers drink beer, like music, and are "really good" in the race car. The one quality that separates Earnhardt Jr. from so many other corporate spokesmen is a magical intangible.

"He's real," says Casso. "He's genuine. What you see is what he is, and he is what he is. He's NASCAR's most popular driver because he's real. People can relate to that. We haven't had to force anything, haven't tried to trick anybody because people can pick up on him being real. People like him don't come along very often. He was our A-plus pick and we were fortunate to get him. We wanted him as a rookie so we could grow along with him."

Junior as a Budweiser spokesman? Brilliant! Junior as a Wrangler jean spokesman . . . following his late father in that role? Brilliant!

Junior as an Enterprise rent-a-car spokesman? Brilliant!

The secret of Dale Jr.'s marketing success is fairly simple: he's genuinely interested in the products he represents. Plus he also happens to be very good at what he does. *Nigel Kinrade*

Junior and Michael Waltrip hawking auto parts for NAPA? Brilliant!

Junior as a (fill-in-the-blank) spokesman? Brilliant!

People who know about such things feel Dale Earnhardt Jr. is the prototypical corporate spokesman. He's well-known, well-loved, and believable. He's young, attractive, and seemingly sincere. He looks like he probably uses what he's trying to sell. He comes across as natural and friendly, the kid next door suggesting you try this hot, new shaving tool.

Almost without argument—and in no specific order—the biggest surnames in racing are Andretti, Earnhardt, Foyt, and Petty. Despite her lack of on-track success—through the middle of 2006, at least—Danica Patrick is Indycar's most marketable driver. (Some feel Marco Andretti's youth, name, and talent will get him there). In drag racing, the stars remain inactive drivers Kenny Bernstein, Don Garlits, Shirley Muldowney, Don Prudhomme and current star John Force.

"But Junior's the big one," says Dave Ferroni, a longtime, Minneapolis-based sports marketer. (His resume includes two stints with the U.S. Olympic hockey team, several years at Brainerd International

Opposite: Dale has become a marketing power through Budweiser, Wrangler and other brands. Who was the last Cup driver with his popularity? Dale Sr., of course. *Nigel Kinrade*

The No. 8 Chevrolet is one of the most recognizable in Nextel Cup racing. Its only rivals might be the 24 of Jeff Gordon and the 20 of Tony Stewart. *Nigel Kinrade*

Dale Jr., in front, and Tony Stewart, on Junior's bumper, have become two of the most competitive and popular drivers in NASCAR Nextel Cup racing. And Budweiser and The Home Depot are getting to run out front. *Nigel Kinrade*

Opposite: All drivers wear caps and uniforms with decals of teams and sponsor, but Dale Jr. has become a true marketer for the many brands he represents. *Nigel Kinrade*

Raceway, and tours with NHRA and NASCAR drivers). "Junior's the Tiger Woods of racing. Michael Jordan was the top man for sports marketing when he was winning all those NBA championships. Tiger's taken over that role, but Junior's clearly the most marketable racer.

"The only person close would have been his father. Junior has everything going for him. He's got the family legacy, he's competitive, he's been successful, and he has a great personality. With even a little on-track success, his name will carry him a long way. No question, Junior's presence builds brand awareness. People stop and watch when he's on TV. They stop and listen when he's on radio. And for now, I don't think it makes a lot of difference whether he wins or not."

Like Ferroni, Larry Camp of Concord, North Carolina, has been involved in motorsports marketing for 20 years. He's studied the sport and the business—separately and as they dovetail—and he feels Earnhardt Jr. is doing exactly what clients want him to do.

"He appeals to the persona his endorsers have identified as their target customer," Camp says. "They've got demographic and psychographic data to back up their decision that he's their best fit. Sponsors always want the 'dream spokesperson,' someone at the height of his popularity who wants to purchase their product. Today's young drivers must have the complete

"He's genuine.
What you see is what he is,
and he is what he is.
He's NASCAR's most popular driver
because he's real."

— *Kathy Casso, Director,*
Budweiser's domestic sport-related marketing

Dale Jr. has won his share of trophies and honors, but fans and sponsors love him in a way that few drivers have experienced. *Nigel Kinrade*

Opposite, top: Dale Jr., in the Oreo/Ritz Chevy, and Paul Wolfe, in the Ragu Dodge, have a food fight of sorts in a 2004 Busch race at Daytona. *Nigel Kinrade*

Opposite, bottom: Dale Jr. races at Daytona in 2004 in the No. 81 KFC Busch car. KFC is one of the many brands that have backed Junior for one or two races during his career. *Nigel Kinrade*

package of looks, personality, ambition, talent, and team chemistry. Long-term, though, the ability to drive a race car is still the most important prerequisite."

Camp suggests that Patrick is closest to Earnhardt Jr. in the marketing arena. "You can't say one is better than the other because they appeal to different cultures," he says. "Danica appeals to a more diverse audience. She appeals to males with her looks. She appeals to independent-minded females who see her as a role model. And she speaks to females who see her as a torch-bearer for women's equality. She's a female in a male-dominated sport, and smart marketers can use that to their advantage. She also plays into the reason most racers are admired: they tempt death every time they strap on a helmet. A woman doing that is especially intriguing to many people."

Will Junior's legion of fans stay loyal through a prolonged drought? Will they support "his" beer and jeans and razors if he never challenges for a Cup? As he grows older and younger drivers take hold—Denny Hamlin, Kasey Kahne, Brian Vickers, and Kyle Busch come to mind—will his fans resist the temptation to move? As history shows—Richard Petty being the prime example—fans generally stay loyal through the peaks and valleys.

"He's the hottest item right now, but there are some others who're close," says Denny Darnell, a longtime motorsports agent and marketing coordinator from near Bristol, Tennessee. "Kasey Kahne (with whom Darnell works). Tony Stewart. Jeff Gordon. Jimmie Johnson. Those guys race good and show up good on TV, so more companies are using them to sell products. Junior's in that group of four or five young drivers who have brand credibility.

"The reason is simple: Advertisers want them to appeal to a younger demographic. Older fans tend to buy the brands they've bought for years; they're not going to try anything new. But that 18-to-35 group is willing to switch brands. I buy what I want and nothing's going to change me. Younger buyers

aren't locked in. They're the customers that companies want. There was a time when Budweiser used Clydesdales and three frogs to sell beer. Now, they use Junior."

Timing (we're told) is everything, and today's crop of 20- and 30-something drivers came in just as many of NASCAR's greatest drivers were heading for the door.

"The guys that older fans grew up with are gone," Darnell says. "Rusty retired. Dale Sr., Davey and Alan Kulwicki were taken from us. Rudd quit for a while. Richard, Darrell, Cale, Buddy, Harry, Bobby, Donnie . . . all those guys retired, too. The younger guys are good on TV and good on the track, which makes them even more attractive. Junior leads everybody in souvenir sales, so I guess that means he's the sport's most marketable driver. But that other group is right there, closing in."

Jade Gurss is the on-site publicist for Budweiser's stock car account. He's worked with Earnhardt Jr. since his rookie Cup season of 2000. Gurss feels that while age is a factor in driver popularity and marketability, on-track performance and personality are equally important.

"Companies want cars and drivers that run up front," he says. "But they also want a personality to represent their product. It's a real balancing act to develop a personality that appeals to race fans and the company's employees. A good example is Western Auto. When it began sponsoring Darrell Waltrip (in 1991), it found that employee retention improved. Its people were excited to be involved in racing with a personality like Darrell.

"If you sat down to develop the perfect driver/spokesman, you'd come up with somebody like Junior," Gurss continued. "The big thing is to be real. Drivers can't fake it and try to fool anybody because they're in living rooms 38 times a year. They've got to be true to who they are, and Junior is. He really likes rock music. He really likes to have a beer with his buddies. He's the real deal on the race track, too. He's the perfect mix."

And he's no sellout. Earnhardt Jr. is a believable spokesman for Wrangler, but he turned the company down when it first pitched him several years ago. "He told them he didn't wear their jeans because he didn't like them," Gurss says. "They asked what he liked, and he told them. They came back within a few months with two or three styles he liked from a new line. He was up-front and honest with them, and that's the kind of guy he is."

Dale Jr. hasn't received many beer showers in victory lane lately, but it apparently hasn't hurt his popularity. *Nigel Kinrade*

With all of the racing and the promotion of products, Junior seems to get few chances to sit in front of a toolbox and relax. *Nigel Kinrade*

Dale Jr., Dale Sr. and the United States of America all go together in at least one fan's mind. *Nigel Kinrade*

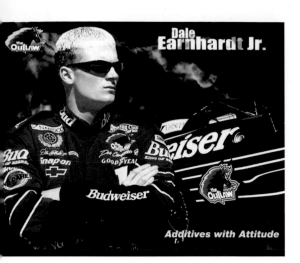

Junior's attitude, cool and brashness have given marketers something solid to work with. *International Motorsports Hall of Fame*

There was no such hesitation when Anheuser-Busch approached Dale Earnhardt Inc. in 1999. The St. Louis–based corporation wanted to "reenergize" its Budweiser brand that had become associated with older customers. In NASCAR and Earnhardt Jr., they found the perfect marketing tool: A young, hip, cool beer-drinker who'd just won back-to-back Busch championships. It didn't hurt that his father had a long relationship with the Busch brand and with the Busch family on a personal basis.

"He's been exactly what we hoped he'd be," says Casso. "We haven't had even a minute's problem with him. He's not bulletproof yet, but he's taken on rock-star status. He's something of an icon in and out of the race car. I think everybody can see him as a real beer-drinking, music-loving, hard racer."

In short, the perfect cat to sell Bud—not to mention those red caps and shirts and jackets and sunglasses and flags and coolers and (fill in the blank)—to those millions of people in NASCAR nation. ●

4

GETTING STARTED

Dale Earnhardt Jr. had Clint Black on the back of his car for the May 24, 1998 race at Charlotte, but he didn't make sweet music. He started 23rd, finished only 175 of 200 laps, and placed 30th. *Nigel Kinrade*

3 ACDelco Clint

NOTHIN' BUT THE TAILLIGHT

"All of a sudden,
you put him in
a piece of equipment
that can run,
damn, he's got some talent."

—Marty Smith

THERE THEY WERE—THREE KIDS WITH THE LAST NAME EARNHARDT—tooling around the Late-Model racing scene, working at their father's Chevrolet dealership, and having a ball.

Kerry was the oldest son, followed by Kelley, the only daughter, and Dale Jr., and despite being the children of racing royalty, they had no more than the average aspiring racer did.

Their father made sure of that.

When the decision was finally made for Dale Jr. to take the step up the ladder that led to NASCAR Winston Cup racing—the NASCAR Busch Series—it almost didn't happen.

"When Dale Sr. decided to give Dale Jr. a chance to drive the Busch car, he only planned a half season," said one person familiar with the story. "I'd love to tell you that Dale Sr. spotted the talent that Junior ended up having, but I really don't think anybody did."

Except maybe Tony Eury Sr., who is Junior's uncle and was the childhood playmate of his father.

Earnhardt Sr. asked his longtime friend and former brother-in-law (both had married daughters of the legendary car builder and mechanic Robert Gee at roughly the same time) if his youngest son would make a driver someday, and the answer, not surprisingly, was, "Hell, yes."

That was in 1995. The following year, things began to percolate for Junior.

Junior made his Busch Series debut in 1996 at Myrtle Beach (South Carolina) Speedway, starting 7th and finishing 14th, a lap down to winner David Green, which was a pretty good result for a kid with hardly any time in the car. He did know the track pretty well from racing late models there, but still, a top-15 his first time out was nothing if not a success.

Driving Dale Earnhardt's No. 31 Sikken's Car Refinishes Chevrolet, Dale Earnhardt Jr. started 18th among 42 cars and finished 7th in a 1997 Busch race at Michigan. *Nigel Kinrade*

"All of a sudden, you put him in a piece of equipment that can run,

damn, he's got some talent.

Then, when he started tasting it,

hell yeah, that's what he wanted to do.

I think he had visions of greatness as a young child; that's all he

knew. That's what his dad was about,

but I don't think it was until he got to the Busch cars

that he realized, 'Hell, I might be able to do something here. I could

make a living at this.'"

—*Marty Smith*

The 1997 Busch Series season was a learning experience for Dale Earnhardt Jr. He ran eight races that year, six for Dale Earnhardt and two for Ed Whitaker, as he prepared for winning the Busch titles in 1998 and 1999. *Nigel Kinrade*

At Myrtle Beach on that June afternoon, it was a beastly hot day. It was the kind of hot you get when you're in the lowlands of South Carolina, too far away from the ocean for it to do any good. Sticky, muggy, and blazing hot. There's no telling what was going through Junior's mind that day, sitting inside the transporter. Was he thinking of what his father would do? His grandfather? Whatever he was thinking that day, it was the start of a career that has, relatively speaking, hardly even begun.

Though it was the only start he made that year, driving his father's car, it was a beginning. By the time he was finished with the Busch Series full-time at the end of his second championship season in 1999, it was a solid beginning.

The following year, with Eury's patient tutelage, he turned 21 and made eight starts in the Busch Series, led 22 laps, finished seventh at Michigan, and otherwise put himself in position for a full-time ride with his father's team. Not that Senior was having any of that, mind you, at least not openly.

When the 1998 season rolled around, it was time for Junior to make good on his promise, shown in the nine Busch Series starts he had made in the two years prior. Senior hemmed and hawed around about hiring a full-time driver for the Busch car until Eury called him out. "Why not put Dale Jr. in the car and invest the money in him?" was the way he put it.

"Junior wasn't doing well in late models because Dale made (Junior) use his own money and get his own sponsors just like (Dale) had to do, and Junior was struggling," Eury told *The Sporting News*. "Dale wouldn't give it to them. But there really wasn't anyone I would have preferred putting in the car at that time." As things turned out, it was a pretty smart decision all the way around.

"I don't know that (Dale Jr.) knows if all he ever wanted to do was race," said NASCAR.COM writer Marty Smith, who is a close friend of Junior's. "I think he wanted to be good at it.

"For the longest time, man, he had every intention of changing oil for a living," Smith recalled. "He felt that was what was in the cards for him. He got a chance to run late models, won a handful of races in 180-odd starts; he didn't set the world on fire in late model cars. Then Tony Sr. went to Big E and said, 'Look, we need to try Dale Jr. in this Busch car.'"

It's February in Florida, which means an Earnhardt will make the annual pilgrimage to Daytona to do battle with the track that is the family's nemesis. *Nigel Kinrade*

Dale Jr. had been racing late models around the Carolinas since 1991, first for Gary Hargett and then for himself. He had fun, but when the call came to start driving the Busch car for his father, it became a business. And what a business it has become, especially since Junior is now the most popular driver—in just about any category you want to mention—in NASCAR.

But when he was 22 years old, he was just Dale Earnhardt's kid, just coming into the legacy that fate and genetics would provide.

"He didn't care as much then," said NASCAR.COM's Smith, who broke into the sport about the same time Junior did. "He was all about the party. It's not that he didn't care about racing; he did, but at that point in his life, it was still about making Daddy happy. It was still about being good enough and achieving enough to make his dad happy."

When he got into the Busch Series car, a light went on in Junior's head, according to Smith.

"All of a sudden, you put him in a piece of equipment that can run, damn, he's got some talent," Smith said. "Then, when he started tasting it, hell yeah, that's what he wanted to do. I think he had visions of greatness as a young child; that's all he knew. That's what his dad was about, but I don't think it was until he got to the Busch cars that he realized, 'Hell, I might be able to do something here. I could make a living at this.'"

All he did with that opportunity was dominate.

Dale Earnhardt Jr. talks to fellow driver Randy LaJoie at a Busch Series race at Talladega on April 26, 1998. Junior won Busch titles in 1998 and 1999, matching LaJoie's two Busch championships in 1996 and 1997. *Nigel Kinrade*

Two races after his Busch Series victory at Texas, Dale Earnhardt Jr. had the chance to get reflective at Talladega. Junior started fourth at Talladega on April 26, 1998, but he finished only 43 of 113 laps and placed 32nd. *Nigel Kinrade*

In his first full-time season in the Busch Series, Junior won 7 of the 31 races, finished in the top five 16 times, and added 22 top-10 finishes to the total. Just three DNFs marred the season—and one came at Daytona, where he crashed; he others for mechanical reasons.

Victories at Gateway, Richmond, IRP, California, Milwaukee, Dover, and, the first one, Texas, showed the rest of the world—and more important, Dale Sr.—that the kid had what it took.

He didn't beat a bunch of underfunded losers for that first Busch title, either. He scraped past Matt Kenseth by 48 points to win the crown.

Smith, who is a media star in his own right, crafted his friendship with Earnhardt the way most get started in racing: by running into each other in the garage area.

"It started as strictly professional," Smith recalled. "His first year in the Busch Series was 1998, and I'd heard a little bit from there, and of course, he was Big E's boy.

"I got hired by NASCAR and my primary responsibility at the time was the Busch Series and the Truck Series, so I would go to all the stand-alone Busch events and whatnot. I got to know him better at that point, see him in the garage. We didn't hang out or anything, but I'd see him around."

Seeing each other around was enough to form the basis of that friendship, and it has grown the longer the two go on.

"As time passed, we started hanging out more and had a lot in common, similar views on things and whatever, and it fostered a really good friendship," Smith said. "Even above and beyond the friendship,

Dale Jr. at Michigan International Speedway on August 16, 1998. That race was a boon for DEI, with all three of the team's car qualifying in the top five, and Dale Jr. on the pole. *Nigel Kinrade*

Dale Earnhardt Jr. had a few laughs with Dale Earnhardt Sr. and Steve Park at Bristol on August 22, 1998. Junior started 4th and finished 15th, four laps down. *Nigel Kinrade*

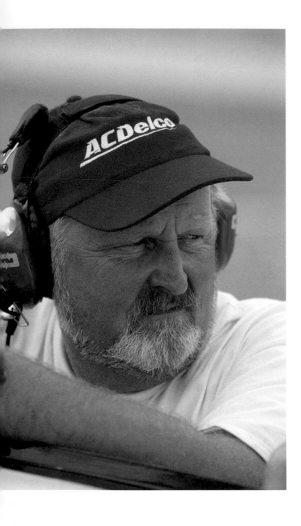

Tony Eury Sr. guided Dale Earnhardt Jr. to a fifth-place start and a third-place finish in the 1998 fall race at Charlotte. It was one of 14 top-10 finishes for the No. 3 Busch team in the last 19 races of the 1998 season. *Nigel Kinrade*

Notice that Dale Earnhardt Jr. wears an open-faced helmet with goggles, just as his father did. Dale Jr.'s third-place finish in the fall Busch race here (Charlotte) was the fourth of five straight top-eight finishes in 1998. *Nigel Kinrade*

Earnhardt Jr. pulls into the pits at the 1998 Stihl 300 held at Atlanta Motor Speedway on November 8, 1998. This Busch race was a star-studded affair, with Mark Martin winning, Earnhardt Jr. placing second, and Tony Stewart on the last podium spot. Earnhardt Jr. left Atlanta with a 166-point lead in the standings. *Nigel Kinrade*

there's a pretty damn stellar mutual respect for each other. He's always been complimentary of me and my work and the way that I do my job. Of course, he's Dale Jr."

That last sentence reveals a lot about what it must be like to be Dale Jr.

"I remember going to (cable sports host) Jim Rome's show when (Dale Jr.) won his second Busch championship," Smith said. "We were in a limo and we were out in Los Angeles for the Busch banquet festivities. We're on the way, and he sort of nonchalantly looks over at his PR people and says, 'Oh, I don't have a belt.' That makes PR people, who are on this strict, stringent schedule, that makes them tear their hair out. But he could get away with it, so he did."

Even if he could get away with small things like that, there was a lot he couldn't get away with, especially on the track. Junior was pushing Jimmy Spencer hard during the last 10 laps of a race at Las Vegas Motor Speedway, and as Spencer recalled, it was a message from Dale Sr. that stopped it. According to Spencer, Senior radioed to his son that there were two people that weren't to be fooled with on the race track, and that Spencer was one of them. The other happened to be Senior himself.

As Junior progressed through his seasons in the Busch car, winning races and championships and slowly growing the legend that would turn into the whole Dale Jr. persona, Junior began to understand some things about the sport and his part in it. The first was perception. In addition to being in the spotlight because of who his father was, he was also finding out that the bright light of media scrutiny shines harshly when it's on you all the time.

"When he burst onto the Cup scene, with all the hoopla of being Budweiser's poster boy, Dale Earnhardt's son, and a back-to-back Busch Series champion, there was a lot of hoopla surrounding Dale Jr.," Smith stated. "Budweiser really played into this young, hip, alternative sort of persona and marketed the hell out of that. Young girls loved him, young guys my age loved him, and when you're at that level of celebrity, there are a lot of extraneous factors involved."

Junior wasn't too many years removed from being painfully shy and introverted, and it was a lot to handle for a kid who was barely able to take a legal sip of his future sponsor's product.

"He's a great guy, but he's not who a lot of people think he is," Smith said. "He's not necessarily what you see on TV. He's not this extroverted, balls-to-the-wall kind of guy all the time. For the most part, he's still very shy, extremely introverted, and he's a tough nut to crack. It takes a long time to sort of enter his circle from the standpoint of being somebody that he truly trusts."

As the fame and celebrity grew, so did the crush of people who wanted nothing more than to get close to the gravy train and ride for free, as Smith pointed out.

"Everybody wants something from you," Smith said of his perception of Junior's life during the period between the Busch championships and his burgeoning Cup career. "Everybody wants to take, take, take, and very few people give back. That's a very difficult position to be in when you don't know who you can trust and you don't know who is in it for what reason. It can be extremely difficult and taxing mentally and psychologically because you're always looking over your shoulder and wondering, 'Is that guy hanging out with me for the right reasons? Does he like me or my money?' That's a hard place to be."

Another thing that Junior had to face as he went from being a pretty good little Busch driver to a pretty good little Cup driver was the unfair notion that he was somehow less gifted because of the way he speaks in public. That's something Smith saw from both sides, both as a member of the media and as a friend.

"The thing about Junior . . . don't get me wrong, he will welcome you with open arms, but getting in there and being able to get in that mind . . . he is an extremely, extremely intelligent individual," Smith said with feeling. "Sometimes when he speaks in public, people perceive his good ol' boy, 'don't make no never mind to me' as unintelligent. That couldn't be farther from the truth.

"Just because he doesn't use perfect grammar or articulate things in a perfectly articulate fashion, there's a misperception and a misconception of his intelligence level. He is extremely smart. He wrote a piece about his dad on NASCAR.COM . . . dude, it was unbelievable. He has this great creative mind."

In all of this, the kid that started out playing with Matchbox cars while his sister Kelley was out being a daredevil developed a boatload of business acumen that has served him well since the death of his father and his entry into the truly stratospheric popularity that was part and parcel of his father's legacy.

"I think he really understands now how this business works," Smith said. "I gave him a lot of credit for his creative mind, but he's also a damn intelligent businessman. He understands what his worth is now in this game. He has won enough races and proven himself worthy of that compensation." •

Matt Kenseth and Dale Earnhardt Jr. are frequent companions on and off the racetrack. While the two drivers are a bit of an odd couple, they share a love of NFL football and heavy metal music, and they came up through the ranks together. *Nigel Kinrade*

5

THE PUBLIC AND PRIVATE JUNIOR

Dale Earnhardt Jr. contemplates life and auto racing in the garage at New Hampshire in 2004. Junior had a good race that year at Loudon, starting third and finishing the same. *Nigel Kinrade*

"If this was the 1950s,
Jeff Gordon would
be Pat Boone and
Dale Jr. would be Elvis."

—Monte Dutton

Dover hasn't been a bad track for Dale Earnhardt Jr., but it's forced him to be thoughtful. The year this photo was taken—2004—Earnhardt posted 26th- and 16th-place finishes at the Monster Mile. *Nigel Kinrade*

IN THE BIZARRE ROAD SHOW THAT IS THE NASCAR NEXTEL CUP SERIES, few stars shine brighter than Dale Earnhardt Jr.'s.

Part of that, as has been explained elsewhere in this book, is his legacy: son of the most revered icon NASCAR has had since Richard Petty, and grandson bred from championship stock on both his father's and mother's side.

Another part of it is his rock-star persona. Junior has been known to hang with some pretty popular people—Kid Rock, for instance—and that breeds some notoriety of its own.

He has a group of friends, consisting of some homeboys and his sister, Kelley, which is virtually impenetrable and very good at screening Junior from the prying eyes of the world at large—except for the news media. That includes television, radio, print, and digital media, as well as photographers and other assorted hybrids. A flock of about 80 travel to most or all of the races, right alongside the teams, officials, and companies involved in the massive traveling road show that is modern-day NASCAR. Indeed, drivers and other NASCAR stars see these media members who cover the race circuit more often than anyone except maybe the stars' own families and teammates.

As such, those folks who cover NASCAR week in and week out have developed some pretty good insight on just who Junior is, not just as a driver, but as a person, too.

Some media members are able to, over time, develop somewhat unique relationships with the drivers they cover. It's inevitable, really, because no one else understands all that drivers and teams and car owners have to go through to make a living.

Besides, when was the last time you met a newsperson who didn't have an opinion or observation . . . on anything?

The ever-quotable motorsports writer for the Gaston (North Carolina) Gazette, Monte Dutton, has seen enough of Dale Jr. to formulate many opinions of the man.

"I think what makes him a popularity dynamo is that he manages to put together a remarkable coalition," Dutton said. "He's both the legacy of his father and the voice of a new generation. I think that, sure, he carries the allegiance of people who were fans of his father, but I also think he's his own man, and he's actually quite different from his father."

It is that very independence, Dutton says, that makes Junior the cultural force that he has become. It is very similar, in fact, to the way Dale Sr. was with his father, Ralph.

"Young people, particularly, like (Dale Jr.) and are drawn to him," Dutton postulated. "One of the reasons is that race car drivers, normally, take the opposite path to maturity. Most people, when they're young, are concerned about appearances, and as they get older they become independent and they basically take the attitude that 'this is why I think I'm right and if people don't like it, I can't help that.' Drivers start out that way, when they are impetuous young hellions at the local short track, and then they get to the top level and get so caught up in being corporate spokesmen and listening to

Martin Truex Jr. (left) poses with car owners Teresa Earnhardt and Dale Earnhardt Jr. the week of the 2004 Busch Series banquet in Orlando, Florida. Truex was the Busch champion in both 2004 and 2005. *Nigel Kinrade*

The 2004 Chicago race was a forgettable outing for Junior—he started 25th and finished 22nd. Tony Stewart won the race, with Jimmie Johnson and Dale Jarrett finishing second and third.
Nigel Kinrade

everyone who tells them what to say, that they end up taking the reverse path. They become more aware of appearances.

"I think one of the things that makes Dale Jr. uniquely popular is that he hasn't managed to succumb to that, that he still calls it the way he sees it, and he actually still has that independence. He basically says, 'This is what I think and I can't control whether you like it or not.' That rings truer than if he were not as independent."

The inevitable contrast to Junior's independence can be found in the initial perception of Jeff Gordon to NASCAR fans in the early 1990s.

"I think he is a marked contrast to Jeff Gordon, who early on just wanted to go racing and said what everyone told him to say," Dutton theorized. "He got a lot of detractors because of that, because everyone figured he was a goody-two-shoes pretty boy. That wasn't ever true, but that early impression plays for him. Dale Jr. didn't have to deal with that."

Dutton went a bit further in delineating the contrast.

"If this was the 1950s, Jeff Gordon would be Pat Boone and Dale Jr. would be Elvis," he said. "There were more Elvis fans than there were Pat Boone fans."

Another reason for Junior's popularity is his ability to stay humble in the face of overwhelming attention, says Chris Economaki, dean of motorsports journalists and the editor and publisher emeritus of National Speed Sport News.

"I don't know him that well, but I wound up at a table with him at the Waldorf Astoria two or three years ago during the annual NASCAR Awards Banquet," Economaki said. "It was during the press conferences, and I happened to be sitting at his table. He's a pleasant sort of fellow, and he's not impressed with his own importance."

Economaki, who was one of the announcers on the first live telecast of a NASCAR race at Daytona in 1960, said that Junior would, in all likelihood, enjoy some relative anonymity.

"I think one thing that has never changed about Dale Jr.,
which he has no problem telling people,
is that he likes to have fun.
If you look at the things, as he has gotten older,
the one thing that remains constant
is that he always finds ways to have fun."

—*Jim Utter*

This sign on the tool box in Junior's garage says it all.
Harold Hinson

"He's a very solid guy and likes what he's doing," he mused. "I think he is . . . upset is too strong a word, but it seems like he'd just as soon do without all the attention that he's getting. A lot of drivers love that stuff, but I don't think that's true of him. He obliges, but not cheerfully."

It is that reservation, for lack of a better term, that has helped grow such a legion of fans, Economaki said.

"I think Dale Earnhardt Jr., because of his reserved nature, that's one reason he has such a huge fan following," he said. "He's no Darrell Waltrip from a standpoint of his public persona; he's not out there talking and making noise about this, that, and the other thing. At the track, he goes back to his motorhome and closes the door. He's not running around making appearances like some others do."

Over his career, which spans nearly 70 years, Economaki has seen virtually every generation of motorsports from the "big car" era of the 1930s to the birth of NASCAR in 1947 to today's skyrocketing roller coaster. He was the PA announcer when Daytona International Speedway held its first race in 1959—it was an Indy car race, surprisingly—and enjoys access as an insider the world over.

He has a theory on why the generation gap is easier to overcome these days.

Tony Stewart, Elliott Sadler, and Dale Jr. confer at Chicago. Sadler ended up mired in the back of the pack. Stewart crashed hard in practice, but put his back-up car to good use to score the win. *Nigel Kinrade*

"Today, I would think it's easier for drivers to live up to their fathers' legacies because of the massive press attention the sport is generating," Economaki explained. "A few years ago, the sport didn't get this kind of attention, and reporters are now running around looking for angles and looking for stories so they stumble onto this second- or third-generation guy, and even though he might not deserve that kind of attention, they write him up."

Such is not the case, however, with Dale Jr. When you have as much corporate "juice" as Earnhardt does, you can be fairly flexible with your time. Sponsors expect drivers to live up to the letter of the contracts they sign, which means that a certain number of appearances must be made on behalf of said sponsor, a certain number of interviews conducted, merchandise signed, and so on.

Drivers like Earnhardt Jr., Tony Stewart, and Jeff Gordon are able to mix that schedule up a bit more than a newcomer or a driver who has less juice. And, in fact, Junior does stay flexible and mix things up, just like his father did before him.

Dale Earnhardt Jr. hasn't had a lot of success at Infineon Speedway in Sonoma, California, but he looks good doing it. In his first six Sonoma races, he finished 24th, 19th, 30th, 11th twice in a row, and 42nd. His average finish there (22.8) is worse than his average start (22nd). *Nigel Kinrade*

Race fans would be thrilled if Dale Jr. could spend all of his time signing autographs. Alas, he has to spend a few hours a week with racing. *Nigel Kinrade*

Dale Jr. was all smiles at the annual media tour at Charlotte. Testing at Daytona went well for the number eight car, and a fresh season of racing was ahead. *Harold Hinson*

Dutton, the North Carolina motorsports writer, says the reason that Junior has been able to live up to and even extend his father's legacy is because of his attitude.

"The reason he's pulled it off is because he's never been a cheap imitation of his father," Dutton said. "He's been proud of his father, but he's been a different person, has a different background, came along at a different time in history, and he's never been afraid to be true to what he is. Oddly enough, that's probably the secret.

"There are many second-generation persons—they don't have to be race drivers; they could be baseball players or bank tellers—who end up succumbing to be cheap imitations of the old man. Many times, a person who finds himself in that position ends up trying so hard not to make mistakes that he can't do anything right. Earnhardt Jr. has always had enough self-reliance to be himself."

Junior's ability to be himself is why Jim Utter of the Charlotte Observer and That's Racing.com feels that Junior is able to survive and flourish in an increasingly busy world.

"I think one thing that has never changed about Dale Jr., which he has no problem telling people, is that he likes to have fun," Utter observed. "If you look at the things, as he has gotten older, the one thing that remains constant is that he always finds ways to have fun.

"At one time, it might have been raising hell with his friends and going to Wal-Mart at three o'clock in the morning. Now, because of his popularity and notoriety, he sort of has to bring the fun to himself,

The best times for Dale Earnhardt Jr. are when he hangs out and laughs with Tony Eury Jr. (right) and his other crewmen. Here, they hunker down to chew the fat. *Nigel Kinrade*

Dale Earnhardt Jr. sports a gypsy look as he listens to Steve Hmiel, the technical director for Dale Earnhardt Inc. *Nigel Kinrade*

such as the many things that he has at his little estate up in the hidden backwoods of Iredell County, or wherever it is. Cookouts, going out on the lake, he loves having his own race team. . . ."

Utter further underscored the fact that drivers spend almost as much of their time around media people as they do their own families by relating that it almost has to be that way given NASCAR's schedule and the year-round nature of the sport.

"We become (surrogate family and friends) kind of by default," Utter said. "I always compare it to the circus, because you see the same people everywhere we go, over and over and over. You can't help but

develop a friendship . . . because we go to the same places to eat, we stay in the same general area, go to some of the same sporting events. The fact that we all live in the same general area in North Carolina, and we all travel to the same places, you spend as much or more time with them as you do your own family."

The initial impression of Junior, as the spitting image of his father on the one hand or the antithesis of him on the other, is borne out by Utter's comment that, once you spend some time around Junior, you pretty much know whether it's a good time to push or not.

That's just like you know not to bug your mother when she's mad at you or to ask Dad for the keys to the car when you've stepped in it big-time.

In other words, it is just one big family, even if no one is related except by commonality of location and vocation. ●

Junior winning the Daytona 500 in 2004 sent the media into a full-on feeding frenzy.
Harold Hinson

6

EARLY SUCCESS

Dale Earnhardt Jr. on May 6, 2000, at Richmond. Richmond was good to his father, who had five wins there, and was also good to Junior in 2000. *Nigel Kinrade*

"He was willing to work for everything he got."

—Andy Hillenburg

AFTER A 1998 SEASON THAT SAW HIM EARN A NASCAR BUSCH SERIES TITLE—in what was originally planned as a part-time season—Dale Earnhardt Jr. had finally burst upon the stock car racing scene. Not as the son of Dale Earnhardt, although that undoubtedly played a large role in zooming his popularity up the scale, but as a driver in his own right.

In 1999, lots of things were happening to Dale Jr. First came the announcement that he would drive five NASCAR Winston Cup races in the Budweiser Chevrolet, numbered 8 in honor of his paternal grandfather, the late Ralph Earnhardt. Part of that announcement was that he would compete for Rookie of the Year honors in 2000. He had made the big time and would join his father in the big leagues.

Through it all, however, were whispers . . . whispers that he was only getting such an opportunity because he was Dale Earnhardt's son, and that he really wasn't ready, that he would choke.

Like hell.

"I met Junior when he was 17 or so, still running street stocks, I think," said Andy Hillenburg, who owns and operates the Fast Track High Performance Driving School near Lowe's Motor Speedway. "He

Dale Earnhardt Jr. won the pole for the spring race at Rockingham in 1999, but he led only three laps and completed only 126 of 197 after wrecking, finishing 35th. *Nigel Kinrade*

Dale Earnhardt Jr. awaits the start of the IROC race on June 13, 1999, at Michigan. Junior, who finished 10th in the Daytona IROC race and 12th at Talladega, led one lap and finished 2nd in the all-star race at Michigan. The winner? Dale Earnhardt Sr., of course. *Nigel Kinrade*

had every opportunity to take advantage of his status and he never did. He was willing to work for everything he got." Hillenburg, who has turned most of his attention to building his own race teams as well as running the school and cranking out cars for NASCAR movies, remembers when Junior came through his school.

"Back then, you didn't have to be 18 to go through the school," he said. "His first time in the big cars and all was at our school at Charlotte. He had all the tools, and he did all right.

"It's difficult to assess whether or not anybody can win a Cup race while going through a driving school, but obviously, he had all the skills. He would have made it whether he came here or not, but hopefully we contributed a few things to the experience level."

That was in the early 1990s, and Hillenburg's recollection proved spot-on. All Junior did once he got his opportunity was win a Busch Series title in his first full season, then back it up with another the following year.

In his first full Cup season he won two points-paying races plus The Winston at Lowe's Motor Speedway and finished second in the Rookie of the Year race to Matt Kenseth.

In 2000, Junior would also do something that had been done just once in the long history of NASCAR—take part in a race against his father and half-brother Kerry at Michigan. The only other time it happened, Lee, Richard, and Maurice Petty were the father and sons to do it.

But before all that happened, he had one thing to do: defend his Busch Series title.

It started slowly. Junior didn't win until Dover in June, 15 races into the season. A broken shoulder blade in a crash during practice at Milwaukee was another setback. Ron Hornaday Jr. qualified his car for him, but Junior took the wheel for the race and finished third. When it ended, the 1999 season yielded 6 victories, 18 top-five and 22 top-10 finishes—and his second series title. In the five Cup races he started in 1999, Junior earned a top-10 and three finishes of 20th or better.

He was ready for his close-up.

"I didn't know if he could win a title right away," Hillenburg said. "I did know he could win races the first season. A title really takes a lot of patience, and that's a hard thing for young drivers, to realize that when you have a seventh-place car, you try to finish sixth, seventh, or eighth with it. He did that a majority of the time and was able to help himself in the championship."

One of the most interesting—and as it turned out, poignant—stories of the 1999 season was Dale Earnhardt Sr.'s commitment to his son's racing career. Though Senior could be a crusty sort at times, there was a hidden softer side to him that came out as he talked about life as a father.

"I do care what people think about me," Earnhardt Sr. said in a 1998 *USA Weekend Magazine* interview. "It goes back to what advice my dad gave me and how he was raised and tried to raise me: When you leave here, all you're gonna have is your name and your word. If that's not any good, then you're not much good. . . . I want to be remembered as much for that as for being a great racer—being a good father, for one, but also a fair person in life, fair to other people."

Well, no one can say that Senior wasn't fair to Junior, especially as the 1999 season got under way at Daytona.

Dale Earnhardt Jr. had reason to smile for the second Busch Series race at Michigan of 1999. Junior started third, led 69 of 100 laps, and collected his fifth of six wins that year. He also won two races earlier, at Gateway. *Nigel Kinrade*

"I guess when you grow up and your dad is your hero and you can go out and be right there with him, whether you get beat a little bit or beat him, just running with him probably meant the world to him."

—*Andy Hillenburg*

The International Race of Champions (IROC) is an all-star series—everybody who competes in it is a champion. Brothers have raced in it—the Unsers, the Allisons—and just one other father and son combination (Al Unser and Al Unser Jr.), but never had the two Earnhardts been on the same track at the same time. Hillenburg had a hand in that, too.

"I helped him when he ran the IROC series the first couple of times," Hillenburg said. "His first year, he had never gotten to run Indianapolis, and the first time he actually raced there was in the IROC cars."

Father and son squared off in the opening IROC race at Daytona and raced together—hard. Though Junior crashed with Indy Car star Eddie Cheever, who had won the Indianapolis 500 the year before— just eight laps into the race, he and his dad spent some time rearranging the sheet metal on each other's cars. Senior won the race by moving Mark Martin out of the way off the final turn.

But it was the third IROC race the two competed in that really rang up some old-fashioned emotion. At Michigan, Senior beat Junior to the line by a scant .007 seconds—still the closest margin of victory in the 30-year-plus history of the series. The two were beating and banging on each other all the way

Dale Earnhardt Jr. races Mike Skinner during the Sept. 11, 1999 Winston Cup race at Richmond. Junior started 21st and finished 10th, one spot ahead of Skinner. Dale Earnhardt Sr., Skinner's teammate with Richard Childress Racing, finished sixth. *Nigel Kinrade*

down the front straightaway toward the finish line. Junior had a run on the high side, and Senior moved up to block. Neither one gave an inch, and they touched. They touched again, and Junior's two-foot lead began to slip away. The last time they touched, Senior squirted ahead and won the race—by two feet. Once they had returned to the front straight, father and son exited their cars and met in a bear hug in front of a packed grandstand.

"That was one of the most unique, neat, exciting, fun—just everything you could describe and roll it all up into one—time I've ever had," Senior said after the race was over.

Someone asked Senior if he should have let the boy win. That earned an Earnhardt snort—and a grin.

"No way," Senior said. "He's going to have to earn everything just like his dad did. I don't think he would have wanted me to let him win. He would have gone home and everybody would have said, 'Your dad let you win.' That wouldn't have been cool.

"Of course, they could say to me, 'Your son let you win it.' Bull. Look at the side of that race car."

Junior was nonplussed, but also proud.

Dale Earnhardt Jr. had a blast at Richmond on Sept. 11, 1999, as he and Dale Sr. both posted top-10 finishes. Dale Sr. was sixth, and Junior ran 10th. *Nigel Kinrade*

Dale Earnhardt Jr.'s pit crew must have done a good job during the 1999 Phoenix Busch Series race. Junior started fifth and finished second in the next-to-last race of the 1999 season. *Nigel Kinrade*

"I was surprised," he said. "That shocked the hell out of me. But, he's supposed to do that. He's got all those years of experience. I was just a sitting duck, right there. It was just tough competition." He went on.

"Today was really special. I can't tell you what it was like to be racing with my dad," Junior said. "There at the end, he seemed to be saying, 'You ain't gonna win, you ain't gonna win it.' That was fun there. I guess you could write a better script," he continued. "I think that was the way it was supposed to be at this point in my career and this point in his career. It ended just the way it was supposed to end. I was trying with all of my might to win that race but that's storybook right there.'

And, as it turned out, prophetic to boot.

"To come down and race side by side, door to door, and finish first and second was pretty awesome," Senior said. "I don't know that we'll ever have that opportunity again, but we did and we experienced it. It's something we're going to cherish."

Senior knew he'd seen something in his son's driving that day that would benefit him in later years—years that he would, sadly, not be there to see.

"I knew he was going to run high and I knew he wanted to try that on the last lap," Senior mused after the race. "I sort of figured out what his mindset was, and I was glad to see him be patient. That shows me that eventually he will win races in that situation."

Hillenburg put it another way.

"I guess when you grow up and your dad is your hero and you can go out and be right there with him, whether you get beat a little bit or beat him, just running with him probably meant the world to him."

At the end of the 1998 season, when the Earnhardts traveled across the ocean to Japan to race in the last of the exhibition races held there by NASCAR, it was built up as a classic first-time event: the two would finally be on the track at the same time, as teammates, yes, but as competitors too.

"The one time I raced against my dad (Ralph Earnhardt) was at a dirt track," Senior said at the announcement of the plan. "I was racing this guy, and my dad, who was leading the race, came up behind me and I couldn't figure out what he was doing. Finally he started bumping me, so I figured I better hold the car straight. He pushed me by this guy and I beat him, then dad drove on past me.

"I got one exciting time racing with my dad and it was pretty neat. I would have liked to have done more of it. It is exciting to see Dale Jr. grow into the sport and it will be a great experience to race him in Japan. However, it wouldn't look very good for him to beat his good old dad, now would it?"

He did, finishing sixth to Senior's eighth.

There's no way of knowing what might have happened had father and son been able to race together for more than a single season, plus seven races.

Two of racing's biggest stars today, Jeff Gordon and Dale Earnhardt Jr., chat at Phoenix in 1999. Gordon led 37 laps and won the Outback Steakhouse 200, with Earnhardt placing second in the AC Delco/Superman Chevy. *Nigel Kinrade*

Dale Earnhardt Jr. talks to Dan Hughes, the QVC television host for *For Race Fans Only*, in Phoenix in 1999. In the background are a No. 99 car and the No. 3 AC Delco/Superman car. *Nigel Kinrade*

At the annual Coca-Cola 600 in 1999, Junior's five-race Cup schedule was announced, and much talk centered on whether Junior, with just two seasons of Busch series competition behind him, would be able to compete at the sport's highest level. There's no question that he could, and can, and will, just as Hillenburg though he could.

Hillenburg still talks with Junior on occasion, but it's getting tougher and tougher to do.

"I don't get to see him much anymore," Hillenburg said. "His schedule is quite the zoo, and mine isn't any better. If he asked me to come over today, I'm too busy!

"Our paths cross, and we talk, but when you get to that status, it's hard. There's not a lot of time to sit around and talk and call up your buddies. He has his little deals up at his place every week, but other than that, I don't think he has a lot of time to make something happen."

Regardless, Hillenburg was and is a big Junior supporter.

"I definitely speak highly of him. It would have been very easy for him to have turned out differently, and he didn't. He's a great guy." ●

Teresa and Dale Earnhardt and others celebrate Dale Earnhardt Jr.'s Busch Series championship in 1999. It was his second Busch title in a row, and he would move up to Winston Cup the next season. Junior finished second at Homestead, his third straight second-place finish. *Nigel Kinrade*

Dale Earnhardt Jr., a left-hander, signs a TV truck at Texas Motor Speedway as cameramen capture the event. Junior started fourth that weekend, led 106 laps, and posted his first Cup victory. *Nigel Kinrade*

Opposite: Dale Earnhardt Jr. gets a beer shower as he celebrates after winning in 2000 at Richmond International Raceway. Junior started fifth, led 31 laps, and won the race. *Nigel Kinrade*

Dale Earnhardt Jr. mentally prepares for his debut in The Winston at Charlotte. Apparently it worked, because Junior won NASCAR's all-star race in 2000, his rookie year in Winston Cup. *Nigel Kinrade*

Opposite: A week after finishing fourth at Charlotte, Dale Earnhardt Jr. walks across the stage at Dover before the race. He started 6th and finished two laps down in 10th place. *Nigel Kinrade*

Opposite: Dale Earnhardt Jr. looks pensive before the Coca-Cola 600 at Lowe's Motor Speedway in Concord, North Carolina. Dale Jr. won the pole, led 175 of 400 laps, and finished a solid fourth in the Cup Series' longest race. *Nigel Kinrade*

Above: A pair of Dale Earnhardts run nose to tail at Pocono. Dale Jr. started 15th, and he finished on the lead lap, but he ran only 19th. Dale Sr. did better, finishing fourth behind Jeremy Mayfield, Dale Jarrett, and Ricky Rudd. *Nigel Kinrade*

Dale and Tony Eury Jr. plot strategy before a race.
Nigel Kinrade

Dale Earnhardt Jr. signs an autograph for one of his legion of fans as he gets ready for the second Michigan race of 2000. Earnhardt won the pole and led 13 laps, but he finished a lap down in 31st place. *Nigel Kinrade*

Opposite: Dale Earnhardt Jr. is near the front of the pits at Indianapolis as more cars enter the pits. Earnhardt had a decent race at Indy, starting 6th and finishing 13th. *Nigel Kinrade*

Dale Earnhardt Sr. was a perennial favorite at Charlotte Motor Speedway, and Junior is well on his way to following in his father's footsteps at the track.
Nigel Kinrade

Dale Earnhardt Jr. isn't a natural on road courses, and his first attempt at Sears Point in Winston Cup was a learning experience. He started 31st and finished on the lead lap in 24th place.
Nigel Kinrade

7
DALE'S DEATH

Dale Earnhardt Jr. rests on his tarp-covered Chevrolet at Watkins Glen.
Nigel Kinrade

"He did a lot of soul searching at that time."

—Marty Smith, talking about Dale Jr.'s reaction to his father's death

MOST PEOPLE REMEMBER WHERE THEY WERE AND WHAT THEY WERE DOING WHEN THEY GOT THE WORD that terrorists in airplanes had hit the World Trade Center on September 11, 2001. NASCAR fans remember that, too. But they also remember February 18, 2001, the day Dale Earnhardt Sr. died. It's a tough call, among fans of the iconic driver, to tell which had the more profound effect.

If it was that way for race fans, imagine what it must have been like for Dale Earnhardt Jr., who was just ahead of his father when his fatal accident occurred, there in the fourth turn at Daytona International Speedway.

Speeding toward the finish line, tucked in behind Dale Earnhardt Inc. teammate Michael Waltrip, Dale Jr. had no way of knowing what was going on behind him, other than his father had crashed with the finish line in sight.

He soon found out, as he sat in the NASCAR transporter with NASCAR president Mike Helton and Ty Norris, then the general manager of Dale Earnhardt Inc. When Dale Sr.'s life ended, a pillar of strength in Dale Jr.'s life had come crashing down.

The tributes to Dale Sr. came pouring in, from NASCAR stars, team owners, and friends, remembering Earnhardt in heartfelt prose.

Dale Sr., Dale Jr., and Teresa at Daytona in 1998. This was a big year for Dale Sr., as he finally found a way to win the prestigious race. *Nigel Kinrade*

Most of the focus was centered on Earnhardt's widow, Teresa, or the family in general. Not many mentioned Dale Jr., even though he had to be mourning just as deeply.

Stevie Waltrip, Darrell's wife, quoted scripture. Kix Brooks and Ronnie Dunn, Dale Sr.'s buddies from country music fame, recalled the times they spent fishing with Senior for blue marlin.

Norris, one of Dale Sr.'s closest advisors and the man hand-picked to run DEI as Senior's lieutenant, recalled his own reaction as one of disbelief, suspended animation intruding on real life with all the sense of a bad horror movie. Norris simply could not believe that Dale Earnhardt was dead. Neither could Dale Jr.

The irony of his father's death, if such a statement can be made, is that Dale Jr.'s grandfather, Ralph Earnhardt, died young as well, and the shock of his passing played a major role in Dale Sr.'s life in terms of drive and the desire to succeed.

In 1998, Dale Earnhardt Jr. was beginning to make a name of his own in the Busch Series. He won titles in 1998 and 1999, with limited appearances in Winston Cup competition. *Nigel Kinrade*

Tony Eury Sr. was an anchor on Dale Jr.'s team in both Winston/NEXTEL competition and during Junior's Busch series days. *Nigel Kinrade*

Opposite: The Earnhardts confer at Bristol in August 1998. Bristol is another signature Earnhardt track, a place where Dale Sr. first made his mark (sometimes literally) on the competition. *Nigel Kinrade*

"I knew Dale's father, Ralph, and I've known Dale since he was a little boy," said Lowe's Motor Speedway president and general manager H. A. "Humpy" Wheeler at the time of Senior's death. "He had things pretty tough when his father passed away when he was young, and I was so proud of the way he turned out and the way he represented our sport."

From wild and untapped to stable and steady, Dale Sr. managed to find his way around the death of his own famous father in 1973. He applied the lessons he learned in helping Dale Jr. grow into the man he would become, especially on the race track.

"It wasn't so much Dale molding Dale Jr. as Dale Jr. wanting to be Dale Jr.," team owner Richard Childress said years later in an interview with *The Sporting News.* "Dale went out and did his thing. But he had someone watching every move he made, and that was Dale Jr. It was just like Dale watching his father, Ralph, race."

So when his own famous father died, where did Dale Jr. turn when it was time to grieve for the namesake he would never see again? A variety of sources, it appears.

One of those was his stepmother, Teresa. Teresa, child of a racing family herself, told Junior to stop being selfish, stop thinking that his father's death was just about him. And it worked, according to Junior.

"If everybody in the world said right there, 'It's all right if you don't [race],' I wouldn't have," Earnhardt Jr. told NASCAR.COM's Marty Smith on the fifth anniversary of his father's death. "I was like, Man, I'm going to the race track, what am I gonna do? How am I going to act?'"

His stepmother asked, in no uncertain terms, that while Junior could wish that Senior was still there and he could miss him, why did he think that Senior's loss was his own private tragedy? The advice stuck with Earnhardt Jr., and his stepmother was one of the first people Junior acknowledged following his own Daytona 500 victory in 2004.

Another person Junior turned to was his sister, Kelley, his partner in nearly all things since birth.

"Junior leans on Kelley, above all else," said Smith, who is a close friend of Earnhardt Jr.'s. "He trusts her more than he trusts anybody in the whole wide world. He's leaned on her his entire life. She has guided and directed him his entire life, and that will continue for a long time to come."

Following the death of their father, it was Junior who consoled Kelley. That was quite a switch from when Kelley did Junior's chores for him when they were kids so Junior wouldn't get in trouble. In turn, Kelley helped Dale Jr. realize that he could indeed make it on his own.

She had gone with him to Oak Ridge Academy, the military school Junior attended in the late 1980s, continuing to protect her younger brother even as the two became adults.

As they grew older, Junior grew out of the painfully shy and retiring shell he presented as a boy and into a more self-possessed young man, a fact his sister recognized on the occasion of her own wedding in July of 2001. Since her father was no longer there to walk her down the aisle, Kelley said, she planned to walk alone. But Dale Jr. stepped up into his father's shoes and performed that most solemn of duties.

"It was awesome to have Dale Jr. walk me down the aisle," Kelley related to Lee Spencer of *The*

Dale Jr. races at Bristol in April 1999. John Andretti won the April Bristol race, and Dale Sr. won the August event after bumping Terry Labonte on the last lap. *Nigel Kinrade*

Sporting News. "It is fitting for our relationship. We are great friends who can share our thoughts and discuss life's challenges without judgment. He respects who I am, and I respect who he is."

Slightly more than five months after his father died—and after a lifetime of unconsciously doing it every day—Dale Jr. took a walk in the shoes of the man whom he'd looked up to and found the journey invigorating.

Of course, the first step back into the race car after his father's death was painful, in more ways than one. On the first lap of the race at North Carolina Speedway, Junior crashed. He didn't complete a lap and finished 43rd. On the other hand, DEI teammate Steve Park won the race, in a storybook ending.

In fact, it would be four more races before Earnhardt Jr. even looked like he was back on track. An eighth-place finish at Texas was his first top-10 since his father's death.

"He's not a very public person at all, and it was very hard, extremely hard," Smith said of Junior's reaction to his father's passing. "He did a lot of soul searching at that time. There are many different examples

that I will keep between Junior and myself, but I can tell you, personally and with great accuracy and conviction, that the soul searching he did was on many levels, those being spiritually, professionally—'Should I be doing what I'm doing, can I ever achieve enough success to carry on my daddy's legacy?'—There was a lot of difficulty there, and I respect what he did even more now than I did at the time, because when you step back and get a little older and you really understand the impact of who his father was, and losing that prominent a figure."

Smith pointed out that the one who had to face the aftermath of his father's death in public was Junior, not Teresa.

Dale Sr. stands beside Dale Jr. as he collects the 1999 Busch Series title at Phoenix. *Nigel Kinrade*

For a short while, we thought we'd be seeing sights like this week to week, with the Earnhardts running nose-to-tail or door-to-door. Alas, it ended too soon. *Nigel Kinrade*

Dale Jr. was riding high in the spring of 2000. Shown here at The Winston, he became the first rookie driver to win NASCAR's All-Star race. *Nigel Kinrade*

"Teresa wasn't around. She didn't have to answer to the media. Junior did. That was very difficult on him. too, from the standpoint that, 'Look, man, I kinda didn't ask for this.' Yet there he was. He put that entire company on his shoulders and made it happen. In the aftermath of his father's passing, he struggled a lot."

Of course, Junior had the "family" at DEI to turn to, but everywhere he looked, he saw his father. All the important people on his team—crew chief Tony Eury Sr., car chief Tony Eury Jr. most of all—were related in some way or another, and that relationship went back to his grandfathers' day.

During Junior's rookie season in 2000, everyone on the outside looked at their performance and saw a coming force. Inside the shop, however, it wasn't at all unified.

Tony Eury Sr., whose father Ralph had raced against Ralph Earnhardt, said the problem was immaturity on the part of both the Juniors—Dale and Tony.

Dale Jr. was an in-demand personality after his Busch Series title win. *Nigel Kinrade*

But then Senior was killed at Daytona and the immaturity was lost in the haze of young men forced to be older than their years.

Through it all, several of Junior's friends from around Mooresville, where he grew up, helped him stay sane and somewhat focused. These are friends Junior has had since before he was Heir Apparent to his legendary father.

"He leans on his buddies," Smith said. "He has a very small group of buddies that have been his buddies since before he was anybody, the Dirty Mo Posse. They're all a bunch of good ol' boys."

Hank Parker Jr., another friend of Junior's, perhaps put it best in an interview with *The Sporting News*. "They keep him grounded, and Dale Jr.'s all about keeping it real," Parker said.

"That's what people like about him," Parker told *The Sporting News*. "He is a real strong and very private person. He knows his friends are just his friends, and they don't want anything. Once you earn Junior's trust, you're his friend forever."

The Earnhardts are nose-to-tail at Dover in 2000, where they finished 16th and 17th, with Junior getting the better of his old man that day. *Nigel Kinrade*

The 2001 Daytona 500.
Nigel Kinrade

Earning Junior's trust means you have to first get past the public face he puts on. The public face is somewhat different from the real Dale Jr., more like the shy little boy his sister says he was once upon a time.

"He leans on the same guys he leaned on his whole life," Smith summed up. "Of course, he enjoys a level of celebrity that very few NASCAR drivers ever have or currently do. Maybe Jeff Gordon (has that level of celebrity) . . . . Jimmie Johnson is getting to a level where the Hollywood crowd understands and

recognizes who he is . . . maybe Tony Stewart, too. Junior is (at) a different level. Everybody wants him and he doesn't give a lot, but those guys that get it, those are his guys."

Instead of a shy and introverted young man, Earnhardt emerged from the fire of the life-shattering events surrounding his father's death both stronger and more vocal about who and what he is.

"There's a lot to be said for that, for a guy who will stand up and just be who he is and who will tell you what he thinks," Smith said. "That's pretty rare and special."

Through the harrowing ordeal that was his father's death, that shy and retiring young man pulled himself up—partly through the friends he had around him and partly by knowing that's the way his father would have wanted it—and out of the misery in which he found himself. ●

DEI drivers (from left) Steve Park, Dale Earnhardt Jr., and Michael Waltrip were thoughtful at Rockingham the week after Dale Earnhardt Sr. died. Dale Jr. started 25th but crashed at the start of the race and finished 43rd. *Nigel Kinrade*

Dale Jr. at the Martinsville race on April 8, 2001. Dale Jarrett won, and Earnhardt's results were forgettable. *Nigel Kinrade*

Dale Earnhardt Jr. had a lot to think about in 2001, including the death of his father and his own rise to the top in popularity. *Nigel Kinrade*

Dale Earnhardt Jr. was still learning his way around Bristol and getting over his father's death when he passed the No. 3 logo on March 25, 2001. Junior started 9th but finished 31st, 44 laps down, at NASCAR's shortest Cup track. *Nigel Kinrade*

Crew chief Tony Eury Sr. keeps a close eye on Dale Earnhardt Jr. at Richmond, Virginia. Junior had a good day on the three-quarter-mile short track, starting 14th and finishing 7th. *Nigel Kinrade*

Dale Earnhardt Jr.'s No. 8 car leads a group of cars through the esses at Sears Point on June 24, 2001. Junior had a decent day, starting 37th and finishing 19th. *Nigel Kinrade*

Dale Earnhardt Jr. and another Dale, Jarrett, have been two of the more successful drivers at restrictor-plate races. Jarrett, though, has three Daytona 500 wins to Earnhardt's one.
Nigel Kinrade

Dale Earnhardt Jr. returned to The Winston in 2001 as the defending champion of Humpy Wheeler's all-star race. The 2001 race was less heroic: he started the first segment 15th and finished the last segment 7th. *Nigel Kinrade*

It wasn't an easy race when Dale Earnhardt Jr. returned to Daytona International Speedway for the first race since his father's death there on Feb. 18, 2001. Still, Junior prevailed; he started 13th, led 11 of 160 laps and won the Pepsi 400. *Nigel Kinrade*

Dale Earnhardt Jr. and his crew had one of the most memorable celebrations in NASCAR history after he won the Pepsi 400 at Daytona. It was the first race at Daytona since Dale Earnhardt Sr. died there on Feb. 18, 2001. *Nigel Kinrade*

Dale Earnhardt Jr. had a pretty good points day at New Hampshire, starting 29th and finishing 9th on July 22, 2001. That left him eighth in the points standing, 417 points behind co-leaders Dale Jarrett and Jeff Gordon. *Nigel Kinrade*

Opposite: Pocono is a 2.5-mile, triangular track that requires some introspection. Dale Earnhardt Jr. had a great day at Pocono on July 29, 2001, starting 12th and finishing 2nd. *Nigel Kinrade*

Road courses aren't Dale Earnhardt Jr.'s cup of tea, but Junior started 27th and finished 12th on Aug. 12, 2001 at Watkins Glen. It was the first of back-to-back 12th-place finishes that season for Junior. *Nigel Kinrade*

Sparks flew in September 2001 during the night race at Richmond. Dale Earnhardt Jr. started eighth, matching his car number, and finished third, matching his father's. Better yet, Junior would win the next week at Dover. *Nigel Kinrade*

Racing wasn't a laughing matter the weekend of the Kansas City race in 2001. Dale Earnhardt Jr. started 22nd, led three laps, crashed, and finished 33rd. He finished 228 of 267 laps. *Nigel Kinrade*

Dale Jr.'s fourth career win came at
Dover Downs in September 2001,
where he led 193 of the 400 laps.
Dale Jarrett was on the pole for the
race, but finished in 12th place.
Nigel Kinrade

Opposite: Dale Earnhardt Jr. appeared to be learning short tracks when he started second at Martinsville, but the Virginia track is a tough place to race. He finished four laps down in 27th place. *Nigel Kinrade*

Sometimes you get the bear, and sometimes it gets you. Like all drivers, Dale Earnhardt Jr. has spent some time during his career being hauled back to the garage after a wreck. *Nigel Kinrade*

Opposite: Junior celebrates with his team after starting sixth, leading 67 laps, and winning the EA Sports 500. Talladega and Daytona have been great tracks for Dale Earnhardt Jr. *Nigel Kinrade*

Jimmie Johnson and Dale Earnhardt Jr. haven't become masters of the road courses, but they've won two of the last three Daytona 500s (2004 for Earnhardt, 2006 for Johnson). *Nigel Kinrade*

Dale Earnhardt Jr. is usually business-like when people—and cameras—are watching, but sometimes he's eager to play around with drivers and crewmen in the garage area. *Nigel Kinrade*

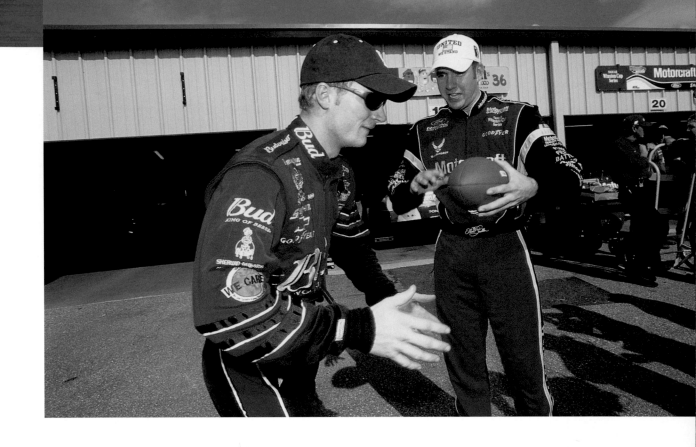

Dale Earnhardt Jr. runs beside DEI teammate Steve Park during the 2001 season-ending race at New Hampshire. Junior started 8th but finished 24th, three laps down on the one-mile track. *Nigel Kinrade*

Richard Childress, left, and
Teresa Earnhardt, right, are
among those celebrating a Busch
victory with Dale Jr. *Nigel Kinrade*

8
TITLE CONTENDER

Dale Earnhardt Jr.'s Chevrolet sprints through the Watkins Glen road course in 2004. Junior started third and finished fifth, one of his 21 top-10 and 16 top-5 finishes of 2004. *Nigel Kinrade*

"It's all about the confidence, you know."

—Dale Earnhardt Jr.

Aᴀꜰᴛᴇʀ ꜰɪɴɪꜱʜɪɴɢ ᴛʜᴇ ᴍᴏꜱᴛ ᴘᴀɪɴꜰᴜʟ ꜱᴇᴀꜱᴏɴ ᴏꜰ ʜɪꜱ ʏᴏᴜɴɢ ᴄᴀʀᴇᴇʀ—and the worst year of his young life following the death of his legendary father, Dale Jr. entered the 2002 season on a mission: win races, win titles, and make his own way in the world.

His third NASCAR NEXTEL Cup season—even though it wouldn't be called that until 2004—began slowly after finishing 29th at Daytona. Just a year after his father had died in Turn 4 on the last lap of the race, as Junior trailed teammate Michael Waltrip to the checkered flag.

At California Speedway in April, Junior hit the wall hard and suffered a concussion. Only he didn't tell anyone else until it was almost Labor Day. That didn't stop him from winning at Talladega in April or again in October, but it did stop him from having a better season.

In 2003, that better season was almost the best, nearly resulting in his first championship.

He finished third in the final standings behind Matt Kenseth and Jimmie Johnson, and if not for the fact that his close friend Kenseth—who had beaten him out for Rookie of the Year honors in 2000—was virtually bulletproof over the final 33 races of the season, Junior might have returned the favor.

Finally, Dale's boy was a threat for the title.

In 2004, the first year of the Chase for the NEXTEL Cup, he was right there again, winning the Daytona 500, three years to the day after his father was killed at the same speedway. It was a triumph, and although he had won at Daytona in the summer of 2001, pulling off a move that would have done his daddy proud, this was the Daytona 500.

Since his father had been so good on restrictor-plate tracks like Daytona, it only followed that the youngster would be as well. Dale Sr. had stocked DEI with the kind of people who knew how to race on plate tracks, and that worked in his favor. Among them was Richie Gilmore, who headed the engine room at DEI.

"It's no secret about Richie Gilmore's success at Daytona, you know," Junior said after winning at Daytona. "He's won five Daytona 500s now with different people, you know they just always have been able to go to Daytona and make a good motor. But Daytona is where he really shines. That was important to Dad and so that was his No. 1 choice. Richie agreed to come on."

Gilmore would move up from the engine room to head all of DEI, running the company for Earnhardt's widow, Teresa, after the departure of the well-respected Ty Norris near the end of the 2004 season.

Part of the DEI chemistry that existed under Norris was the emphasis on good engines and good aerodynamics, Junior said. Old friend Richard Childress, for whom his father drove and won six of his seven titles, was part of that too.

"We got into that RAD program with Richard Childress (and Andy Petree) years ago, and that was a big beneficiary to DEI because we gained instant knowledge that Richard and his team had developed for years," Junior remarked. "We incorporated so many fabricators into our program. One year, we had 5 fabricators. And the next year 10 and now we have our own fabricating department. It's just a madhouse over there. It just keeps growing, every year you need more fabricators. You can't just plug anybody into that department. They have to have knowledge, you know, understanding. Every guy has got to know every piece that he makes is critical and how to make it the best he can."

Another part of that equation was the Eury family, Tony and his son Tony Jr.

"Tony Sr. and Tony Jr. have always built speedway cars," Junior said. "Tony (Sr.) won five in a row with Dad in the Busch Series at Daytona, so they learned as they went and applied what they learned every chance they got. That car we built when we were rookies and went down there (Daytona) wasn't really that great, but Michael (Waltrip) took the same car and won with it last year at Talladega. It just takes

time to build on something, improve it, and keep working on it. Eventually, when you have all the right people, you'll figure it out."

Despite the fantastic season that 2004 turned out to be, it was not without problems.

In July, during on off-weekend from NASCAR, Dale Jr. crashed the Corvette he was testing for an American Le Mans Series race at Infineon Raceway in California. The car burst into flames with Earnhardt still inside. He suffered second- and third-degree burns on his neck, chin, and legs. The burns prevented him from finishing two races so he was replaced by Martin Truex, Jr. (driver for Chance 2 Motorsports, co-owned by Dale Earnhardt, Jr. and his stepmother Teresa Earnhardt) and his DEI teammate (John Andretti) in the middle of the races.

Dale Earnhardt Jr., here leading Tony Stewart across the start-finish line, would have cherished a victory at Daytona one day short of the anniversary of his father's death. Instead, he started 5th and finished 29th, 29 laps down. *Nigel Kinrade*

Dale Earnhardt Jr. worked well in corners at Bristol on March 24, 2002. He started 23rd, led 181 of 500 laps, and finished a terrific 4th on NASCAR's shortest Cup track. *Nigel Kinrade*

In the eighth race of the 2002 season, Dale Earnhardt Jr. had reason to smile. He started a lucky third, led 41 of 500 laps, and finished fifth. The next week he won at Talladega. *Nigel Kinrade*

Opposite: Sometimes a driver sticks his nose in a book while he keeps a low profile in his garage stall. It appears that Dale Earnhardt Jr. is doing that here. *Nigel Kinrade*

Dale Earnhardt Jr. drove just three Busch Series races in 2002, including one in the Nilla Wafers Chevrolet for Richard Childress Racing. Junior started 11th, wrecked, and finished 36th at Charlotte. *Nigel Kinrade*

Speaking of Truex, Dale Jr.'s Chance 2 team made a late run and clinched the NASCAR Busch Series title at Darlington. The title gave Junior three Busch Series championships—his own in 1998 and 1999, and Truex's in 2004.

In 2005, when everything else was breaking up around him, Chance 2 won another Busch Series title with Truex and crew chief Kevin "Bono" Manion.

At the end of the 2004 Cup season, however, all the right people were feuding with each other. What happened after that season was very nearly the undoing of Earnhardt Jr. and his hopes for a championship.

After winning a career-best six races, and leading the points after the third race of the Chase until a poorly timed choice of words in Victory Lane at Talladega cost him 25 points and the lead, it certainly looked like the juggernaut that was DEI was ready to make big noise.

Going into 2005, it was almost a foregone conclusion that Earnhardt Jr. would battle again for the title. Almost.

In an effort to create a better environment at the shop and at the track, it was decided to mix things up.

Eury Sr. was promoted to team manager, overseeing both the No. 8 Budweiser Chevrolet and the sister NAPA machine of Waltrip.

Eury Jr. went from being the crew chief for Junior to Waltrip, taking the No. 8 team with him. Waltrip's team went to Junior's car with Junior's Busch Series crew chief, Pete Rondeau, at the helm.

"It's all about the confidence, you know," he said, with the boyish charm that has captivated millions of race fans.
"You've got to get all that confidence built up, and once you get a full tank of confidence man, you're hard to stop and it's hard to beat you."

—*Dale Earnhardt Jr.*

The Nilla Wafers Chevrolet looked nifty on the Lowe's Motor Speedway racetrack in 2002, but, alas, Junior was fated to wreck and finish just 83 of 200 laps. *Nigel Kinrade*

In hindsight, it probably looked like a good move. Through the crystal-clear prism of history, however, it was a colossal failure at the track and in the shop.

Rondeau led Junior's team through the Coca-Cola 600 before being replaced by Steve Hmiel, the team's director of research and development. Things were a little more stable after the change, and the team did win at Chicagoland on fuel mileage and pit strategy, but Hmiel, a top-notch crew chief for Mark Martin at Roush Racing, was not the long-term fix.

The long-term fix, of course, was Eury Jr.

After Earnhardt Jr. was eliminated from title contention on Labor Day at California, it became obvious that Eury Jr. and Dale Jr. would be reunited. A few weeks later, it was announced, and thus the period of mixing up had come to an end.

Dale Earnhardt Jr. found time to race Ryan Newman at Dover, but he had a neutral race. He started 30th and finished 30th, 4 laps down in the 400-lap race.
Nigel Kinrade

Of course, it didn't come in time for Junior to salvage what is currently his worst season on record. He was 19th in the point standings with just the one victory at Chicagoland.

The 2005 season might have been a total wash had it not been for the combination of events that led to the reuniting of the Juniors.

All the momentum built up through the 2003 season and the 2004 season had been stalled by a clash of personalities among family members. The enforced separation was just what the doctor ordered, but it did not come without its cost.

Expectations being what they are, it was a tough pill to swallow for Junior.

"I don't really know exactly what those expectations are," he said. "But I know that they are high. I know that people want us to win or expect us to win, expect me to be a contender, you know, week in,

Dale Earnhardt Jr. listens to fellow driver Jimmie Johnson in the Pocono garage area. In the 14th race of the 2002 season, Junior started 14th and finished 12th. *Nigel Kinrade*

The Bud crew sends Dale Jr. back into battle as Old Glory snaps in the breeze. *Nigel Kinrade*

A crewman for the No. 8 Dale Earnhardt Inc. Chevrolet team makes sure Dale Jr. has his ducks, er, hoses and lines, lined up correctly. *Nigel Kinrade*

week out, and, you know, there's a lot of variables. There were a lot of variables in my dad's day. He had sort of up and down years earlier in his career, trying to get with the right program, the right people, and all of the sudden he got with Richard Childress Racing with a good group of guys, Kirk Shelmerdine and all those guys and they all clicked and it all worked out.

"Judging on the years before 1996, he wasn't the sole reason why those guys won all those championships. It came down to every one of them having some sort of a talent and some way to fit the pieces to the puzzle together. You know, that sort of plays a lot into it, just like last year, we struggled. I felt like I had a great team, it was confusing and hard to figure out why we could not win races and run better than we did because I felt like the guys that I had were winning guys. I felt like every one of them had enough, if not more, talent than we needed to win races. I just don't know why we couldn't put our car up there where we needed to be and why the car didn't drive like it should.

"There's a lot of things that play into winning races and being successful year in and year out. I think Tony Junior is one of the best crew chiefs in the business. I think that will be recognized years down the road after his career is over with; that he was one of the good ones, and I guess I just try to stick around and try to feed off of that as much as I can and win as many races as I can with him, and try to get that championship. Because, I mean, we all—I feel like I can win a championship. I'm a good enough race car driver. So basically that's what we just focus on, is go out and win races and win that championship."

Building back up and contending again for a title are the main focuses for Earnhardt and his merry band. It will take time, he said.

"I feel like we're one rung low on the ladder as far as championship contender goes," he said. "We're right there. We've just got to get a little better footing. But I feel like we're right there.

"When you go there and expect to win, expect to run the top five, and it's not happening, you sort of have to take what you can get. I've got to use my head and take what I can get in those situations. I think the cars and the team and everything is there for me; when I'm ready to match the gas, it's all there."

Before he won at Chicagoland, his last victory was at Phoenix in 2004. Victories don't come as often these days as they might have in the past, but Earnhardt Jr. knows that victories are the key to getting where he wants to go.

"Winning races is—always going to be a challenge, especially as the competition level in this sport sort of increases across the board. Everybody that rolls up to the race track, 90 percent of the teams have an opportunity and the equipment to win, and it gets harder every year. I don't know, it's going to be tough. But I think we can be there and I think we can make the Chase. I think we can be competitive in the Chase when the Chase comes. So I just can't make the mistakes that I make, and I've got to give my team an opportunity to improve my race car later in the race and try to get something out of it."

Junior sees the key to winning races and being a contender as having to do with confidence, the sort of swagger that the DEI team had in 2003 and 2004.

Dale Earnhardt Jr. has grown mightily as a driver and personality over the last few years, but he still has a thoughtful look while he's talking. *Nigel Kinrade*

"It's all about the confidence, you know," he said, with the boyish charm that has captivated millions of race fans. "You've got to get all that confidence built up, and once you get a full tank of confidence, man, you're hard to stop and it's hard to beat you. If you can get a victory early, you can go into the rest of the season with a little bit more confidence and go to those places where you haven't had a lot of success in the past.

"That's what we're going to need to go in there with, a lot of confidence, to be able to try to do better."

Being Dale Earnhardt's son has never been easy for Dale Jr. It is a tall order to live up to your family name when your family is known for racing. Like Kyle Petty, Dale Jr. grew up in the long, tall shadow of his famous father, never knowing if whatever success he had was because of his own talent or the inevitable benefits that being a scion of stock car royalty often bring.

One of the most painful incidents of that particular paradox came at Daytona in July 2001.

It was the first time Junior had returned to the track that took his father's life since that awful day, and he had to come to grips with it in his own way. He did, driving a Chevrolet Corvette down into Turn 4 by himself and communing with the place—along with whatever ghosts remained.

The all-star paint scheme didn't seem to do the trick for Junior at Chicago in July 2003, as he was out on the 211th lap and scored a 38th-place finish. *Nigel Kinrade*

Opposite: Dale Earnhardt Jr. and Tony Stewart are two of the biggest stars on the NEXTEL Cup Series. And they both favor dark sunglasses on occasion. *Nigel Kinrade*

Later that weekend, he went from sixth to first in one lap and won the race in thrilling fashion.

It was a fantastic story and nearly too good to be true, which some of the more conspiracy-minded of NASCAR's fans latched onto with unseemly fervor.

Earnhardt Jr. was wounded by such considerations, and it showed.

"I think they (skeptical fans) know better," he said. "I don't know . . . it is a shame that people don't have anything better to do but I guess you would have that with anything anytime anybody succeeds at anything. There are going to be some doubters and some people that criticize it no matter what.

"Some people . . . just can't leave well enough alone and enjoy their own life. They have to try and mess and screw somebody else's, but I don't know. I don't really get upset about it myself. But there isn't much I can do about it other than go on and keep on winning and keep on enjoying my own life."

Part and parcel of being a championship contender is facing the fact that a large cross-section of the fans you encounter on a daily basis are really hoping their favorite driver kicks your butt week in and week out. Just ask drivers like Jeff Gordon, Tony Stewart, Jimmie Johnson, and Kurt Busch.

Darlington Raceway was a pretty good place for Dale Earnhardt Jr. in 2003. He finished 6th at the track "too tough to tame" in the spring and 12th in the fall. *Nigel Kinrade*

Dale Earnhardt Jr. and his No. 8 crew have turned celebration at Daytona International Speedway into a science, whether it's the Daytona 500, the Pepsi 400, or a 125-mile qualifying race.
Nigel Kinrade

This special paint scheme coated the No. 8 for the 2003 Busch Race at Daytona. *Nigel Kinrade*

But none of those drivers have the legacy that Earnhardt Jr. does. The sheer volume of his popularity, even when his father was alive, guarantees that some will consider whatever he does to be far short of his legendary parent.

It's a lesson that Earnhardt has learned well, despite the fact he isn't all that comfortable with it.

"Well, regardless of the situation, you're always going to have some people that pretty much despise what you do and what you're about," he reflected. "I guess you just hear it from different angles . . . I don't really get on the Internet and read too much, unless I just won the day before.

"You know, (2005) was every hater's opportunity to really throw stones if they wanted to and a lot of them did. We were down and out and struggling, and, you know, it was probably (that) I heard it more through the grapevine, like things that were said to my team. A lot of those guys had been working with Michael.

"And I told them, when the season started I said: 'Man, when you put that red shirt on, it's going to be a little different.' And I don't think they really knew what I meant until they walked in and out of the

Dale Earnhardt Jr. had mixed results at Daytona International Speedway in 2003. He finished 36th in the Daytona 500 and 7th in the Pepsi 400. He led 43 laps in the summer race to match a pretty good Daytona car number. *Nigel Kinrade*

Dale Earnhardt Jr. broke out the pirate flag for a victory lap after winning the Koolerz 300 Busch Series race at Daytona in February 2003. It was the second of his four straight Busch wins at Daytona. *Nigel Kinrade*

garage, before or after a race and would hear some of the things that fans (would say) . . . because there's an opportunity for all of the fans that didn't like Dale Junior or didn't like the Bud team to come out and get them and get an opportunity to slang toward them, and they did. They were real hard on them boys and that was something they really didn't expect."

In the midst of what became his worst season as a Cup driver, it was one more brick on the load Junior had to carry.

"I've got a big 'ol core group of fans and they totally, you know, overshadow all of the things that you hear from people or hear somebody said about you or whatever," he said. "When I have a bad weekend, I get letters about how to keep my head up and keep digging and everybody is behind me . . . I mean, the people that are not my fans, they are not going to write me and tell how happy they are that I didn't run good.

"I read the letters that are positive and I listen to the fans after the race when I run in the top 10 and they say, 'Man, that was a good run.' Those are the things that are cool. Obviously when you win a race and everybody is happy; but when you put in a hard day's work and you run fifth or eighth or whatever and it was a good hard effort and the fans appreciate it, that's more of a compliment to me that they spent their money, came to the race and their driver ran well and they are happy."

But it's still hard for him to hear the stuff that came his way—and his team's way—during the 2005 season.

"You know, last year was a hard year for the team, and for me," he said. "There were a lot of things said to my team leaving a lot of tracks that I heard about later that were hard for me to imagine. If I were there, it would have been tough for me to listen to and for those guys to walk back in the next week after all that (was said to my team) meant a lot to me. They were still behind me and still getting after it, even after the things that they had to go through on some occasions."

That right there, that loyalty, more than anything else, is why 2006 promises to be the year that 2005 could have been had so many things not gone wrong for the entire Bud team. ●

Ricky Rudd and his team in 2003, the Wood Brothers, were old school when Dale Earnhardt Jr. and DEI were getting established in the Cup series. This photo was taken at Dover, where Junior posted 11th- and 37th-place finishes in 2003. *Nigel Kinrade*

Dale Earnhardt Jr. and Matt
Kenseth have had a strong and
healthy rivalry since they joined
the Cup series, and Kenseth is
ahead of Dale Jr. in some ways.
Junior is the biggest name in the
sport now, but Kenseth was Rookie
of the Year ahead of Earnhardt,
and he won a Cup championship
in 2003. *Nigel Kinrade*

Dale Earnhardt Jr.'s number is 8, of course, but the No. 3 will haunt him the rest of his life. Many fans would like to see Junior drive a black No. 3 for Richard Childress Racing. *Nigel Kinrade*

Dale Earnhardt Jr. leads a line of cars down a straightaway at Watkins Glen in 2003. Junior had his best road-course finish to date in 2003, starting sixth and finishing third behind winner Robby Gordon and runner-up Scott Pruett. *Nigel Kinrade*

Dale Earnhardt Jr. had an undistinguished race at Homestead in the 2003 Cup season finale. Junior started 24th and finished 38th in the race. He placed third in season points for the last Winston Cup championship, though. *Nigel Kinrade*

Dale Earnhardt Jr. and cousin Tony Eury Jr. were tuned in at Martinsville in 2003. The No. 8 team started second and finished third in the spring race and started third and finished fourth in the fall. *Nigel Kinrade*

Dale Earnhardt Jr. has become the most popular person for driver interviews, and the SPEED Channel did its share of talking to Earnhardt in 2003. Here, Bob Dillner asks the questions. *Nigel Kinrade*

Dale Earnhardt Jr. won two races and had two chances to pose with Miss Winston in 2003. This victory obviously came on Nov. 2, 2003 at Phoenix International Raceway. *Nigel Kinrade*

Opposite: Dale Earnhardt Jr. shined in the desert in the 34th race of the 2003 season. Junior started 11th at Phoenix, led 87 of 312 laps, and posted his second victory of 2003. *Nigel Kinrade*

Brothers Kerry and Dale
Earnhardt chat before a Busch
Series race at Talladega in 2003.
Dale Jr. won both Talladega
Busch races that year, and Kerry
started 17th and finished 12th in
the race on April 5. Junior ran
only three Busch races that year,
winning all of them. *Nigel Kinrade*

Dale Earnhardt Jr.'s crew works under the lights in The Winston All-Star Race at Lowe's Motor Speedway in 2003, while a NASCAR official keeps a close eye on the action. *Nigel Kinrade*

Dale Earnhardt Jr. during qualifying at Atlanta Motor Speedway in 2004. Earnhardt posted 1st- and 33rd-place finishes at the Hampton, Georgia, track that year. *Nigel Kinrade*

The pace car pulls off the track, and Dale Earnhardt Jr. leads the field across the finish line in a 2004 race at Bristol. *Nigel Kinrade*

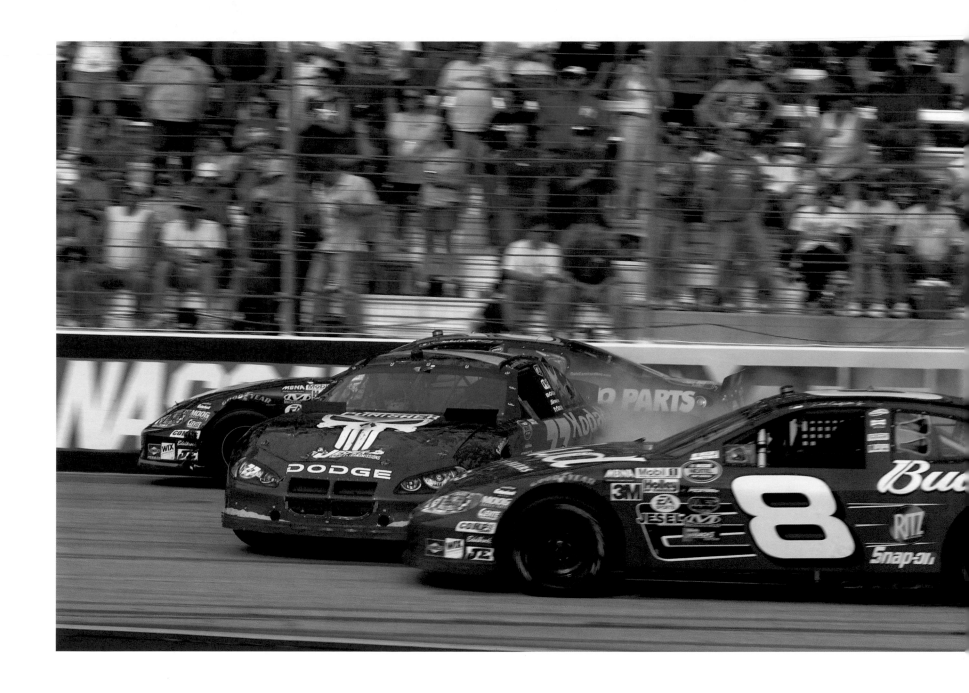

The No. 77 Dodge, driven by
Brendan Gaughan, spins just in front
of Dale Earnhardt Jr.'s Chevrolet at
Bristol in 2004. In the second Bristol
race of 2004, Earnhardt Jr. won the
race, and Gaughan finished 35th.
Nigel Kinrade

Dale Earnhardt Jr. posted one of his best finishes ever in 2004, starting first and winning at Bristol in the No. 81 Busch car. *Nigel Kinrade*

Dale Earnhardt Jr. and Elliott Sadler had a lot to talk about at Chicago in 2004. Sadler finished 21st in the Tropicana 400; Earnhardt was 22nd. *Nigel Kinrade*

Two Dale Earnhardt Inc. crewmen work on the right-rear tire well on Dale Jr.'s Chevy. The race—and the damage—were at Darlington in 2004. *Nigel Kinrade*

Dale Earnhardt Jr. talks to fellow driver Jamie McMurray at Darlington in 2004. Richie Gilmore, the engine builder for Dale Earnhardt Inc., sits between them and listens. *Nigel Kinrade*

Dale Earnhardt Jr.'s biggest on-track moment so far came in 2004, when he won the Daytona 500. On Feb. 15, 2004, the Earnhardts joined Richard and Lee Petty and Davey and Bobby Allison as father-son duos to win the Cup's biggest race. *Nigel Kinrade*

Dale Earnhardt Jr. wears his Busch uniform at Daytona in 2004, when Junior ran Busch races. He won at Daytona and Bristol, placed second at Talladega, and 17th in the other Daytona race. *Nigel Kinrade*

Dale Earnhardt Jr., in the Oreo/Ritz Chevy and Paul Wolfe in the Ragu Dodge have a food fight of sorts during a 2004 Busch race at Daytona. Earnhardt Jr. won the spring Busch race at Daytona and finished 17th in the summer. *Nigel Kinrade*

Dale Jr. in the pits at Daytona in 2004, where the number was skinned with the "Born on Date" paint scheme. Dale Jr. had a great run at 2004 Budweiser Shootout, finishing second.
Harold Hinson

Dale Earnhardt Jr. leads Terry Labonte through a turn at Martinsville in 2004. Earnhardt posted six top-10 finishes and six top-5s in his first 13 races at the short track, but he finished 3rd and 17th, respectively, there in 2004.
Nigel Kinrade

Junior gets a Budweiser shower in victory lane after winning the first 2004 race at Richmond. In the second race, Earnhardt finished second, and Jeremy Mayfield celebrated the victory. *Nigel Kinrade*

Two fans display their support—
and their Budweiser and Dale
Earnhardt Jr. caps—during a
2004 race at North Carolina
Speedway in Rockingham.
Nigel Kinrade

This Bud's all over you, Dale Earnhardt Jr., as he celebrates a 2004 victory at Phoenix. Dale Jr. started 14th, led 118 of 315 laps, and posted his sixth win of 2004. It was welcome, since Earnhardt had crashed in the previous two races at Martinsville and Atlanta. *Nigel Kinrade*

9

WHERE
HE GOES
FROM HERE

After spending much time contemplating his future, both
as a driver and as part of his namesake's team, Dale Jr.
finally had some things to look forward to as the 2006
season dawned in Daytona. *Nigel Kinrade*

"His birthday is something
I do enjoy pointing out
or celebrating."

—Dale Earnhardt Jr.,
talking about his Dad's birthday

As the 2006 season dawned in Daytona, a sense of renewal was on the mind of Dale Earnhardt Jr.

After a bruising and confidence-draining season in 2005, the coming season promised to be, if not a championship-winning season, then at least an improvement over 12 months of hell and damnation that 2005 turned out to be.

Dale Jr. was back with his cousin, Tony Eury Jr., and the rest of the Budweiser crew that had been such a potent force in 2004, when he made a serious run at the NASCAR NEXTEL Cup championship.

Eury Jr. had come back as Junior's crew chief for the last 10 races of 2005, and the reunion proved to be a good thing for both men.

Michael Waltrip was gone as Earnhardt Jr.'s teammate, and young Martin Truex Jr. was in. Dale Jr.'s cars were back to the way he liked them, and he was headed to Daytona International Speedway, where he'd won the Daytona 500 two seasons prior.

Life was finally good for Junior.

"Well, you always emphasize improving," he said during testing at Daytona, two weeks before the start of Speedweeks. "I felt like it was a good opportunity to get to work with Tony Jr. those last 10 races. He had learned a lot of stuff in the setups and his setups were a little different than what I had normally been racing on. And he was, you know, curious as to how I was going to like the things that he was doing with his car. So that seems to be working out pretty good and we really are getting along really good. (There's) a lot of good communication between (us)."

The question has been posed that maybe the horrible 2005 season was really a blessing in disguise. It broke down some of the tension that had permeated Dale Earnhardt Inc., beginning at the end of the 2004 season, and the disappointing season focused the main mission for both the driver and the crew chief: win races and championships.

"If you end the season on a real sour note and morale is low, you're not going to carry a whole lot of momentum throughout the off season" Earnhardt Jr. said.

"So I was glad to be in the position I was last year at the end of the year. We really were ready to race even more. We did not want Homestead to be the last race of the season. We knew that we wanted to go to a couple more races and work together some more and try to learn more. So I felt like that sense of urgency was good and that it carried over throughout the off season. A lot of work, a lot of good craftsmanship and diligent work on the cars was done. Everybody was really motivated and took a lot of initiative to do their job, and I feel like equipment-wise, I couldn't ask for anything better.

"When I look at my cars, the motors have improved, the engine department has found some speed and is still working on even more, so that's good. I just like working with people who are never satisfied and that always continue to try to improve. Even if they look across the board and see that their product is the best, I still want them to keep trying to improve on it. I feel like that's where we're at right now, which is really good."

Two weeks later, he and the Budweiser team went to Daytona and left with an eighth-place finish.

The Bud Boys were back in town.

Of course, restrictor-plate tracks like Daytona had always been a DEI hallmark. The late Dale Earnhardt Sr. was phenomenally talented at both Daytona and Talladega, and he had built his organization around performing well there.

The second race of the year would be the first true test of the renewed team's new chemistry. While Daytona was a test of horsepower and aerodynamics, the second race of the season was at California, where the two-mile distance tests engine, driver, and aero just a little differently.

Dale Earnhardt Jr. holds an introspective pose at Atlanta Motor Speedway in 2005. Atlanta was a mixed bag for Junior in 2005; he started 35th and finished 24th in the 4th race of the season and started 17th and finished 4th in the 33rd race of the year. *Nigel Kinrade*

Dale Earnhardt Jr. and Michael Waltrip, Junior's Dale Earnhardt Inc. teammate, race under the lights at Charlotte in 2005. Junior posted 15th- and 28th-place finishes at Lowe's Motor Speedway that year. *Nigel Kinrade*

Dale Earnhardt Jr. races the No. 81 Menards Chevrolet under the lights in a 2005 Busch race at Daytona. He finished 3rd in February in the Oreo/Ritz Chevy and 40th in July in the Menards Chevy in 2005. *Nigel Kinrade*

Add to that the fact that in the midst of this rebirth, the Chevrolet Monte Carlo SS had a new nose and tail, and you've got the makings of some confusion.

"We tested this car a little bit last year before the end of the season and I felt like the new nose (was) a little bit better," Junior said.

At California, Junior led again and finished 11th, rising to 5th in points. It was the highest he'd been since the second race of 2005.

The third race of the season was also out west, at Las Vegas Motor Speedway. In 2003, Dale Jr. and his team were so bad at Vegas they parked the car after just 35 laps, disgusted and disgruntled.

In 2006, Vegas was better, but not by much. Junior completed the full 270 laps, finishing 27th. While the result wasn't what they'd hoped for, it was at least encouraging.

According to Junior, it was all about working together.

"I think that however you run here is . . . a good way of being able to tell what kind of car or team you're going to be," Junior said. "I'd like to be faster, we're sort of right in the middle of the charts

right now and I think that we can we definitely improve. We definitely need a couple of 10ths, but I feel confident in Tony Junior and the guys that between our communication and everything, we'll get the cars dialed in."

There are many 1.5-mile tracks on the circuit and others that race just like them. Performing well on them was a main priority for Junior and his team.

"I was really happy with how we ran at a lot of tracks last year (in 2005)," Junior said reflectively. "The car that I had at Chicago (for example) . . . was very competitive all day.

"At Homestead, we were really one of the faster cars after 30 laps. But for the first 10 or 15, we were one of the worst cars. So that's like an air pressure issue . . .. Goodyear has several different types of tires that they run at each track, and each tire, each configuration . . . has its little tricks and you have to figure those out for whichever track and whichever tire to be able to get that speed right off the bat. You'll see guys like Martin . . . go out and run in the 31-second bracket, you know, the first couple laps of a run here today. As they fall off typically like everyone else, they have found a good four tenths to

As usual, Daytona International Speedway was a good place for Dale Earnhardt Jr. in 2005. Junior started 5th and finished 3rd in the Daytona 500 in February and started 39th and finished 3rd in the July Pepsi 400. *Nigel Kinrade*

The electronic media descended on Dale Earnhardt Jr. in force for the 2005 Fontana race, in which Dale Jr. had a rough day. In the second race of the 2005 season, Earnhardt started 40th and finished 32nd, 13 laps down. *Nigel Kinrade*

half a second over the field and to start the run. So for 10 or so laps, they are gaining that much time on you, it's really hard to come back and be able to run them back down.

"So we just have to figure out a few things to gain that kind of speed. We tested at Texas and we were really, really fast. I know that the weather and the track conditions were as good as they could possibly be, as good as you could ask for. So we understand that that would improve our speeds a little bit. But as far as the times were, I was really happy with that."

One track that Dale Jr. has never had problems racing on is Atlanta, and he didn't disappoint in the fourth race of the season. A third-place finish, behind Kasey Kahne and Mark Martin, was just what the doctor ordered. Junior was still in the top 10 in points and solid.

Bristol brought another 11th and a one-spot rise in the points, and as the first of two short-track races in a row, it was welcome.

Perhaps the biggest surprise of the season came the following week, the first week of April, when he contended all day for the victory at Martinsville, eventually finishing fourth behind Tony Stewart, Jeff Gordon, and Jimmie Johnson.

To get that fourth-place finish, it was a total team effort. Involved in an early crash that tore the entire right front fender off his car, Junior reached up, pulled the belts tight and raced right back to the top five.

"The target is to run as good as you can every week," he said. "Everything else kind of takes care of itself."

What a difference from the sour, often bewildered statements of the year previous.

Martinsville was, in a word, healing for Earnhardt Jr. and the rest of his bunch. It was a return to big-picture racing that had gotten him within shouting distance of the 2004 series title.

"I think big-picture racing, you'd rather have the fenders on it," Junior joked. "We just kind of came back. We got lucky that the car was still competitive after being in a couple accidents . . . you just take the car you got, do the best you can with it every week, just work really hard, and keep working. When the car's not doing what you want it to do, just keep working. You try till the very end to get it to do what you want it to do."

In a nutshell, that was 180 degrees different from most of 2005.

At Texas, Junior was 12th, and at Phoenix he was 23rd. At Talladega, Junior blew an engine and finished 31st.

Talladega especially was a little hard on Earnhardt Jr. and the rest of DEI, as the race fell on the weekend of what would have been his father's 55th birthday. In honor of his father, Junior and the rest of the DEI cars ran a special black paint scheme that brought tears to the eyes of some of Earnhardt Nation's faithful.

"I think the car looks good, and I think it's a cool way to honor my dad," he said. "It's going to be a lot of fun to be behind the wheel of that car, and sort of see the reaction it gets."

But underneath the fervor of the special paint scheme, there was a hint of sadness. Earlier in the year, on the fifth anniversary of his father's death, he was beset by questions from all sides.

He seemed more at ease with the special paint scheme, which honored his father's birthday instead of the day he died.

"I think his birthday . . . it's really just personal choice in what your opinion is personally," Junior said at Talladega. "His birthday is something I do enjoy pointing out or celebrating or recognizing myself personally because that was always a lot of fun with him when he would get a little bit older we were always picking about what his real age was. But, I don't know, there were some things that come and go without a blink of the eye, but there are other things that come and go that you want to point out and you want to recognize and you do appreciate and you do miss or you do want to—between me and my family or whatnot, and all of his fans, you do want to take a moment and remember. I think his birthday is a good one."

Though he blew an engine and finished well down in the order, if you expected the Budweiser team or its driver to lie down, you would have been wrong.

"His birthday is something I do enjoy pointing out or celebrating or recognizing myself personally because that was always a lot of fun with him when he would get a little bit older we were always picking about what his real age was."

—*Dale Earnhardt Jr., talking about his Dad's birthday*

Dale Earnhardt Jr. leads a pile of cars into the turn during the 2005 Brickyard 400 in Indianapolis. *Nigel Kinrade*

Inset: Dale Earnhardt Jr.'s Chevrolet looks like a crumpled piece of paper 62 laps into the 2005 Brickyard 400 at Indianapolis Motor Speedway. Earnhardt started 27th, crashed, finished only 62 of 160 laps, and finished 43rd—his worst NEXTEL cup finish of the season. *Nigel Kinrade*

The following week at Richmond International Raceway, Earnhardt Jr. took the Bud Chevrolet to Victory Lane for the first time since July of 2005 at Chicagoland. He led the last 45 laps and held off rookie Denny Hamlin to earn his 17th career victory.

At last, the team had come full circle, from contender to confusion to contender again.

"I think we are there," he said following the race. "We keep taking our shots, but we're pretty competitive. Everything is working really great. I couldn't ask for any position on this team to be any better.

"I'm just glad to be back in Victory Lane. It feels really great."

Unlike his last victory, which he sort of backed into on fuel mileage, the triumph at Richmond was a team victory through and through, and it showed how far he and Eury Jr. had come in their own personal relationship.

Their much-publicized split at the end of the 2004 season was, in Junior's words, a way to save their relationship. When they got back together again for the last 10 races of 2005, it showed that the missing trust had been found.

Two sons of famous racing families, Dale Earnhardt Jr. and Casey Mears, chat the week of a 2005 race at Pocono. Mears beat Earnhardt in both Pocono races that year, finishing 14th to Earnhardt's 33rd in the first race and 21st to Earnhardt's 32nd in the second. *Nigel Kinrade*

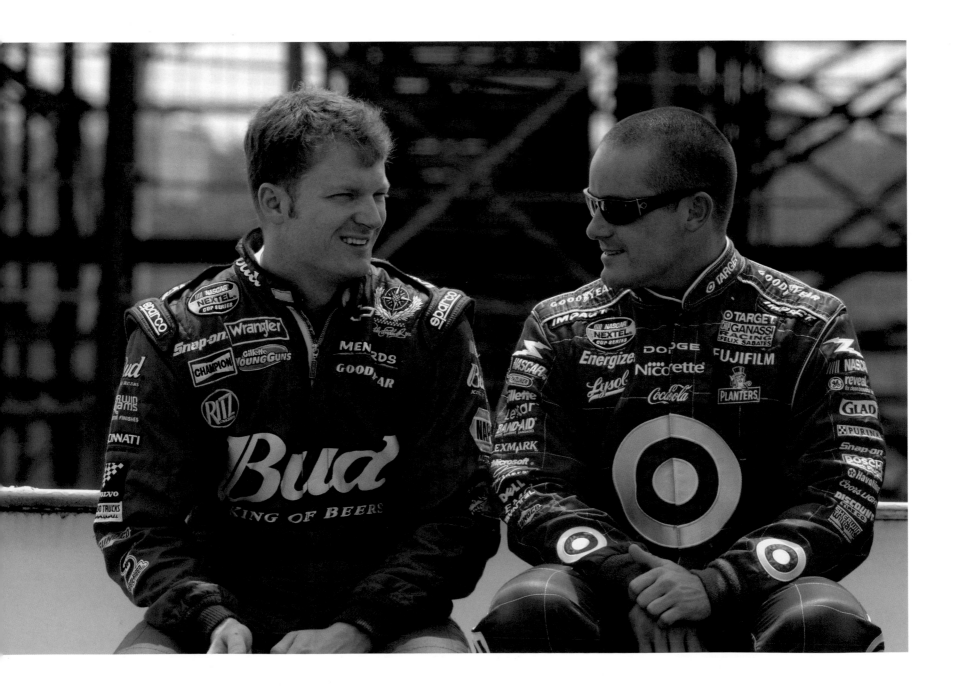

"Well, you know when it comes to the setup of the race car . . . I've got a lot more faith and confidence in what he's putting underneath my car," Junior said. "And I think that he believes or takes to heart everything I'm saying and tries to use that as information more so than we had in the past. You know, we're both just showing each other a lot more respect when it comes to the two things. When I'm talking about the car and when he's putting the setup under there or wanting to make a change, I'm going with it 100 percent. There's no doubt in my mind that it's not going to—it's going to—there's no doubt in my mind it's not going to work.

"We're going to try to maintain that respect because that's sort of the key to keeping each other happy. You know, when we start to get frustrated with the car, sometimes the car sort of . . . is your worst enemy when it's not doing what you want it to do, or when you're driving it and you're not getting around a corner like you want to and when he puts a spring in the right front and it doesn't do what he wants it to; that could be a deciding factor on whether you're both kind of on the same page or you're both

Dale Earnhardt Jr. has improved on road courses the last few years, but he had little luck at Sonoma, California, in 2005. He started a solid 10th, but he completed only 88 of 110 laps and finished 42nd—next-to-last. In his first six races at Infineon Raceway, he finished 24th, 19th, 30th, 11th, 11th, and 42nd.
Nigel Kinrade

As his father before him did, Dale Jr. likes to run the season-opening NASCAR Busch Series race at Daytona. He brought this Oreo-sponsored car home to a 17th place in the Hershey's Kissables 300. *Nigel Kinrade*

At Daytona, Dale Jr. showed some of the old DEI magic during the 500. Here, he uses the high line to get past Brian Vickers (25) and Matt Kenseth (17) on his way to an eighth-place finish. *Nigel Kinrade*

getting along that weekend. So . . . when we don't get results that we want in practice . . . one of us has got to get out and sort of pat the other on the back and put your nose back to the grindstone a little bit and try to get it back where it was."

A lot of the disagreements the two used to have had a lot to do with the pressure on Junior as the son of a legend and as the most popular driver in NASCAR.

Now that the respect between driver and crew chief is back in place, that pressure isn't any less. It's just easier to deal with.

"I go to every racetrack with a lot of confidence. I think it shows my team has got a lot of confidence. That makes me confident when they are confident . . . and I believe that this is going to be the time that

we go there and run good like we should and you know we try to get those results, and I just try to keep my confidence all the time. That was pretty much what I needed to do on my end of the bargain, and my determination showed outwardly instead of just kind of keeping it all in."

As this is written, Junior is solidly in the top 10 in series points and well on his way back to the Chase. He's a little older, a lot wiser, and more able to deal with the pressures of being Dale Earnhardt Jr.

His journey to the promised land of NASCAR legendhood is by no means complete, and despite the trials and tribulations he has endured—the death of his father, the hopeless quest that was his 2005 season, and the everyday effort it takes to be one of the most recognized athletes on the face of the planet—he's still a young man.

There will be plenty to write about in the future, you can count on that. ●

Dale Jr. shares a laugh with Casey Mears prior to qualifying at Martinsville. Junior battled hard all day long, overcoming significant damage to the right front of the Budweiser Chevrolet to finish fourth in the DirecTV 500. *Nigel Kinrade*

After decent runs in the first several races of 2006, Dale Jr. really began to shine at Martinsville. Despite an early crash that left pieces of the Bud Chevy all over the track, Junior and his Bud teammates regrouped to finish fourth. *Nigel Kinrade*

It's a good thing that aerodynamics really don't matter all that much at Martinsville, as a banged up Dale Jr. leads a gaggle of cars through the tight corners on the .526-mile oval. *Nigel Kinrade*

Kevin Harvick was the class of
the field at Richmond, but Dale
Jr. drove into Victory Lane that
night to break a 10-month
winless streak and complete his
turnaround from a miserable
2005 campaign. *Nigel Kinrade*

Getting 2006 started on the right foot was critical for Dale Jr. and the entire Budweiser team. Here, he crosses the finish line third behind winner Denny Hamlin (11) and good friend Tony Stewart at the season-opening Budweiser Shootout at Daytona International Speedway. *Nigel Kinrade*

What a difference a year makes. Dale Jr. (left) and Tony Eury Jr., shown here talking before the start of the Crown Royal 400 at Richmond, needed a year apart to grow up and grow closer, and that year apart has paid off big-time. Later that night, the two cousins would be celebrating in Victory Lane. *Nigel Kinrade*